SECOND EDITION

A Practical Guide to
Finance and Budgeting

Skills for Nurse Managers

KT Waxman, DNP, MBA, RN, CNL

Core Skills
for NURSE MANAGERS
A TRAINING TOOLKIT

HCPro

A Practical Guide to Finance and Budgeting: Skills for Nurse Managers, Second Edition is published by HCPro, Inc.

ISBN: 978-1-60146-136-0

KT Waxman, DNP, MBA, RN, CNL, Author
Rebecca Hendren, Senior Managing Editor
Jamie Gisonde, Executive Editor
Emily Sheahan, Group Publisher
Laura Godinho, Cover Designer
Mike Mirabello, Senior Graphic Artist
David Clemente, Layout Artist
Audrey Doyle, Copyeditor
Lisa Banks, Proofreader
Darren Kelly, Books Production Supervisor
Susan Darbyshire, Art Director
Claire Cloutier, Production Manager
Jean St. Pierre, Director of Operations

Advice given is general. Readers should consult professional counsel for specific legal, ethical, or clinical questions. Arrangements can be made for quantity discounts. For more information, contact:

HCPro, Inc.
75 Sylvan Street, Suite A-101
Danvers, MA 01923
Telephone: 800/650-6787 or 781/639-1872
Fax: 800/639-8511
E-mail: *customerservice@hcpro.com*

Visit HCPro online at: *www.hcpro.com* and *www.hcmarketplace.com*

Contents

A Practical Guide to Finance and Budgeting, Second Edition   www.StrategiesforNurseManagers.com   ©2008 HCPro, Inc.

ABOUT THE AUTHOR

KT Waxman, DNP, MBA, RN, CNL

KT Waxman, DNP, MBA, RN, CNL, has more than 20 years of experience as a nurse leader. She is currently the president and chief nursing officer for KT Waxman and Associates, her healthcare consulting firm in the East Bay area of California. She has held positions as senior consulting manager, chief operating officer, vice president of patient care services, director of behavioral health services, director of critical care services/respiratory therapy, and department director of medical/surgical units. She has a master's degree in business administration and a bachelor's degree in healthcare administration from the University of La Verne in California. She is currently in the process of acquiring her doctorate of nursing practice at the University of San Francisco.

Waxman is a nationally known speaker on the topic of nursing leadership and has presented hundreds of sessions throughout her eclectic career. She has written several articles on the topic of nursing entrepreneurship and leadership. She is an active member of the American Organization of Nurse Executives and has served on several committees. An active member of the Association of California Nurse Leaders, Waxman has served on its board for five years and is a past president (1998–1999). She is currently a faculty member of the California Center for Nurse Leadership and teaches healthcare finance in its intensive program for nurse leaders. Currently the health careers mentor for Monster (*www.monster.com*), Waxman has a passion for mentoring new nurse managers and feels that the middle manager role is the most difficult in healthcare.

How to use the tools on the CD-ROM

Benefits of *A Practical Guide to Finance and Budgeting: Skills for Nurse Managers, Second Edition*

This book guides new managers through producing, presenting, and defending the departmental budget. The CD-ROM is packed with forms, critical thinking activities, and helpful handouts to help meet your financial responsibilities throughout your career.

Versions of the book's tools and templates can be found on the accompanying CD-ROM, as well as bonus tools and cheat sheets. Put your organization's name on the forms, customize them to fit your needs, and print them out for immediate staff use.

How to use the files on your CD-ROM

To adapt any of the files to your own facility, simply follow the instructions below to open the CD. If you have trouble reading the forms, click on "View," and then "Normal." To adapt the forms, save them first to your own hard drive or disk (by clicking "File," then "Save as," and changing the system to your own). Then change the information to fit your facility, and add or delete any items that you wish to change.

The files in the CD-ROM have been organized by chapter in the book. In the folder for each chapter, you will find tools relevant to that chapter.

The following file names on the CD-ROM correspond with tools listed in the book:

File name	Document
Chapter 2 folder:	
Fig 2.1	Sample balance sheet
Fig 2.6	Sample income statement
Fig 2.10	Sample cost center report
Chapter 3 folder:	
Fig 3.10	Updated position control for med-surg/telemetry unit
Fig 3.13	Calculating the number of shifts needed per 24 hours
Fig 3.14	Calculating the number of shifts allowed per 24 hours
Fig 3.24	Budget for medical-surgical/telemetry unit
Fig 3.26	Labor Management Institute: Best practices position control
Chapter 4 folder:	
Fig 4.6	Sample variance report
Chapter 5 folder:	
Fig 5.1	Sample business plan for a medical-surgical unit

The following file names are bonus tools found only on the CD-ROM:

File name	Document
Chapter 1 folder:	
NMChst	Nurse Manager cheat sheet
Srvskills	Five financial survival skills for nurse managers
Chapter 2 folder:	
ISTerms	Key income statement terms
Terms	Key balance sheet terms

Chapter 3 folder:

BudCal	Sample budget calendar
BudForm	Three basic budgeting formulas
CapAcq	Sample capital acquisition request form
CrtThk	Critical thinking
Defbud	Defending your budget
NevSay	Things you should never say to the CFO
OrEdTr	Questions for budgeting orientation, education, and training

Chapter 4 folder:

Prod1	Sample productivity tool (HPPD only)
Prod2	Sample productivity tool (HPPD/CPUOS)

Chapter 5 folder:

Timeline	Sample timeline

Installation instructions

This product was designed for the Windows operating system and includes Word files that will run under Windows 95/98 or greater. The CD will work on all PCs and most Macintosh systems. To run the files on the CD-ROM, take the following steps:

1. Insert the CD into your CD-ROM drive.

2. Double-click on the "My Computer" icon, next double-click on the CD drive icon.

3. Double-click on the files you wish to open.

4. Adapt the files by moving the cursor over the areas you wish to change, highlighting them, and typing in the new information using Microsoft Word.

5. To save a file to your facility's system, click on "File" and then click on "Save As." Select the location where you wish to save the file and then click on "Save."

6. To print a document, click on "File" and then click on "Print."

Chapter 1

LEADERSHIP DIMENSIONS AND PROCESSES

Learning objectives

After reading this chapter, the learner will be able to:

- Identify the flow of the revenue cycle in your facility
- Discuss the foreign language of finance

Today's nurse manager

There is no question that in today's healthcare environment the role of the nurse manager is very different than it was 25 years ago. Back then, nurse managers were referred to as "head nurses" and were responsible for leading their area or unit in a much different capacity than is expected today. Head nurses were primarily responsible for providing patient care and running the unit and were often considered working supervisors. Fast forward to the present and the term head nurse is virtually extinct.

This is not to say that the duties of head nurses no longer exist; on the contrary, they have multiplied. Now you find those responsible for overseeing the same tasks as head nurses donning titles such as nurse managers, directors, coordinators, and service-line leaders, with each title dependent on the hospital in which they work.

These leaders, regardless of their titles, are responsible for managing and guiding their units 24 hours a day, seven days a week. Nowadays, additional skills beyond the clinical base are necessary to do the job. This book will discuss and explain one of the necessary skills for the successful nurse manager: financial management.

Responsibilities

The authority and responsibilities of nurse managers differ from organization to organization. However, there are some core competencies that consistently are required of you. Interpersonal skills, resource management, time management, communication skills, and a clinical background are all part of the nurse manager's repertoire.

Some of the essential functions expected of the nurse manager include the following:

- Develop a practical annual budget for a unit or department that includes volume, revenue, personnel, supplies, and capital equipment

- Give weekly or monthly reports of budgetary variances to your supervisor and review end-of-year data with the finance department and the chief nurse executive (CNE)

- Ensure proper, efficient operations and monitor trends regarding staff, material, and supply usage

- Communicate fiscal management expectations and outcomes to your staff and other stakeholders

Education and training

The majority of the nurse manager's education focuses on clinical nursing. Because you have picked up this book, it's safe to assume that you are just one of the many clinically proficient staff nurses who have been promoted to nurse manager without any formal or informal business or financial experience or training. This side of nurse managing likely causes the most strife and warrants the most education.

Whether you go out and get this training or your hospital makes it available to you, learning the skills necessary to be a manager is vital to your career. To become a successful financial manager, you must know and learn tasks such as creating and presenting budgets, reading financial statements, and managing the financial aspects of the units.

Of course, this is not to say that you should forsake your clinical training. On the contrary, use it to your fullest advantage. As a nurse with business acumen and finance knowledge, you will carry a particularly important position, because you can inject your clinical knowledge into the budgeting process. By doing so, you help ensure that patients continue to get safe, quality care even when budget cuts must be made. To do so, begin by learning what makes the financial hearts of hospitals and healthcare organizations tick.

This is a business

Now that you are a financial manager, the main point to remember is that hospitals and other healthcare organizations are businesses. And for businesses to be successful, they must make a profit on the goods or services they offer or sell.

Many hospitals are not-for-profit. Such organizations generally use earnings to construct new buildings, provide raises for staff, or buy new equipment. For-profit hospitals essentially spend their earnings on the same things; however, they have the additional expense of paying back shareholders.

As with every business, there are certain politics that dictate hospitals' operations. Therefore, you, as a financial manager, must understand the politics behind healthcare economics.

The politics of healthcare economics

Many factors affect the cost of healthcare today. Both nationally and at the state level, the number of people who are uninsured or underinsured is on the rise. More than 47 million people went without health insurance in 2006, including 8.7 million children, according to data released by the United States Census Bureau in 2007.

The state of the economy plays a large role in increasing healthcare costs. During rough economic times, many consumers must make the harsh decision of whether to put food on the table or pay for healthcare. As you can imagine, many neglect their health until they are ill, entering the healthcare system through the emergency department, which increases costs significantly.

Another major factor in increasing healthcare costs is the overall shortage of healthcare workers in the nation—particularly RNs. When hospitals have high RN vacancy rates, they must resort to alternatives such as using costly contract/agency staff and offering incentive programs such as sign-on bonuses. They also use traveling nurses, those on a minimum 13-week assignment, to fill open slots within hospitals at a higher rate of pay. These actions are short-term solutions and significantly increase hospital expenditures.

Technology and pharmaceuticals

The cost of technology plays a major role in the cost of healthcare, and there has been an explosion of available technology in the past 20 years. The more technology that is available, the more there is a need for specialists to run the technology. Hospitals, competing for the best physicians to come on staff to attract more patients, buy expensive technologies.

In the past, hospitals were paid by the various health insurers each time a procedure was performed with new equipment. Today, with managed care and diagnosis-related groups (DRGs), procedures are not reimbursed separately; rather, the hospital receives a flat-rate reimbursement, thus increasing the costs of healthcare.

Hospitals feel it is necessary to have the most current technology to attract patients and physicians, but it can be costly. In addition, with increased litigation in the industry, physicians are more apt to order pricey, high-tech tests to ensure they have covered all bases to avoid a lawsuit. They essentially order tests for the benefit of the medical record, not for the patient.

The number of new medications developed in the pharmaceutical industry has skyrocketed over the past 20 years, thus increasing the cost of healthcare. As these drugs are available and used by physicians, it adds to the costs of patient care. This is because the costs to develop, test, and approve new medications are high, and it can take years before a medication reaches the marketplace. When the medication is finally available to the public, manufacturers must charge enough to cover these costs and pay their stockholders, who expect to see a return on their investment. The price of drugs does not drop significantly until companies begin to sell generic versions of a high-priced drug (National Coalition on Health Care 2007).

Healthcare spending

Understanding how the United States spends its money on healthcare and how it relates to the gross domestic product (GDP) is important. Figure 1.1 from the Centers for Medicare & Medicaid Services (CMS), Office of the Actuary, National Health Statistics Group 2007, shows the national health expenditures and their share of the GDP, 1980–2015. This information provides a big-picture perspective of how expensive healthcare is—and is becoming! National health spending is projected to increase as a share of GDP over the next decade.

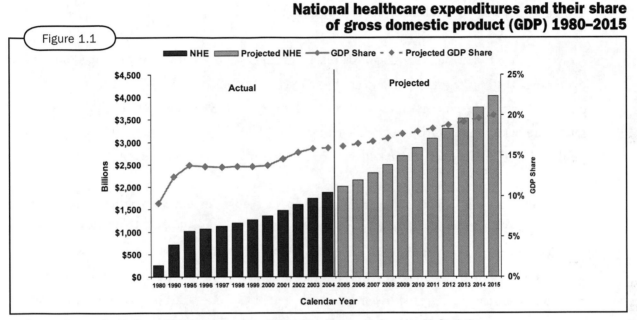

National healthcare expenditures and their share of gross domestic product (GDP) 1980–2015

Figure 1.1

Source: Centers for Medicare & Medicaid Services, Office of the Actuary, National Health Statistics Group 2007. "An overview of the U.S. Health Care System Chart Book." Available from www.cms.gov.

Resources are limited, reimbursement is decreasing, and it has become imperative that nurse leaders control and/or manage costs on their units.

This big-picture perspective affects healthcare costs on a national scale. Each state has its own challenges and issues, and reimbursement by payer type may differ. In 2005, healthcare spending in the United States reached $2 trillion, and that amount is projected to reach $2.9 trillion in 2009 (National Coalition on Health Care 2007).

As the baby boomer generation ages, approximately 77 million people will begin to use healthcare services, and we can expect the related healthcare costs to continue to skyrocket.

The financial reimbursement breakdown

Prior to 1983, hospitals were reimbursed for the services they provided by insurance companies or directly by the patient. This included such expenditures as room charges, nursing care, ancillary services, medications, procedures, linen, food, etc. Bills were sent to the insurance company or patients. This system depended heavily on the nursing department and ancillary services. Cost containment was not an issue: The more hospitals charged, the more revenue they brought in. Management decisions such as the amount of staff or resources were essentially no-brainers because reimbursement was so healthy. Costs were shifted to insurance companies and patients while hospitals enjoyed healthy financial statements.

However, after 1983, Medicare diagnosis-related groups (see p. 4) drastically changed hospital operations. DRGs categorize patient care by characteristics, such as diagnosis, treatment, age, and sex, to estimate patients' approximate length of stay (LOS) and use of hospital resources. DRGs are based on the prospective payment system (PPS), which determines the amount hospitals can charge (hospitals cannot charge for all costs incurred for patient care).

Under PPS, hospitals could no longer charge for costs they incurred. Rather, their reimbursement relied on predetermined prices set by the DRG. Because of this shift in reimbursement practices, many hospitals began providing patients with the lowest level of care possible to control costs. With approximately 700 DRG categories, hospitals are paid a flat-rate reimbursement on the discharge diagnosis regardless of the patient's LOS, tests, procedures, or the supplies used. As a financial manager, you must know how much it costs your hospital to care for patients per day because the reimbursement may not cover the cost of care. Also, depending on the percentage of Medicare patients admitted and cared for, the hospital's bottom line can be negatively affected.

Other payers followed suit, and in the mid to late 1980s, insurance companies also began paying hospitals differently. As mentioned before, insurance companies were billed for services rendered, for which they would pay the hospital. Today, these important third-party payers no longer reimburse hospitals for services rendered: Rather, they base reimbursement on negotiated rates, contracts, and outcomes. These payers often constitute the majority of revenue for hospitals. Some methods of reimbursement from insurers include reimbursing a percentage of the charges, or a "per diem rate." The per diem rate is a negotiated rate that the hospital receives for reimbursement regardless of the actual amount for services rendered. A healthy payer mix composed of primarily third-party payers has a great effect on organizations' financial health. Hospitals with a large percentage of Medicare patients need to make an extra effort to control costs; however, there are times when Medicare actually pays more than some of the hospital-negotiated contracts.

Another significant payer is Medicaid, the state health insurance program for the medically indigent. Under Medicaid, services paid vary from state to state. Reimbursement is often paid at a flat rate.

Changes in 2008

Beginning in October 2008, CMS has announced that Medicare will stop paying for eight reasonably preventable hospital-acquired conditions. This ruling is primarily due to the increasing concentration by payers on quality, patient safety, and hospital performance. CMS has established eight conditions in which the presence of complications and co-morbidities, should they occur during the hospital stay, will no longer lead to a higher DRG payment. The eight conditions are as follows:

- Object left in patient during surgery
- Air embolism
- Blood incompatibility
- Catheter-associated urinary tract infection
- Pressure ulcer
- Vascular catheter-associated infection
- Mediastinitis after coronary artery bypass graft
- Hospital-acquired injury, which includes fractures, dislocations, intercranial injuries, crushing injuries, and burns

As a manager, it is important to continually educate and monitor staff to ensure competency in all areas of responsibility. As you can see from these changes, mistakes can be costly.

Managed care

With the passage of the Health Maintenance Organization Act of 1973, alternative prepaid health plans began cropping up around the nation. By the mid 1980s, "managed care" entered the healthcare arena, and hospitals were forced to adapt to a new reimbursement method.

Managed care refers to the entire spectrum of available alternatives to the traditional fee-for-service mechanism used for provider reimbursement. It is a system that manages or controls healthcare costs by carefully monitoring resource utilization and, therefore, shifting the financial risk to hospitals. In other words, managed care puts the burden of managing costs on hospitals by expecting them to control the use of resources in order for them to receive optimal reimbursement rather than having third-party payers, such as the patient or insurance company, pay for services rendered.

Remembering the various abbreviations for the following managed care plans can be confusing, as there are many. For instance, there are HMOs, IPAs, PPOs—and the list goes on.

HMO

The most common form of managed care is the health maintenance organization (HMO). There are two types of HMOs:

1. The group model, in which physicians are actually employed by the HMO
2. The individual practitioner association (IPA) model, in which physicians maintain a private practice while serving both HMO and non-HMO patients

With both models, a population of patients, or "members," is enrolled for a prepaid fee known as the capitation charge. HMOs focus on preventive care with the ultimate goal of keeping members healthy and out of the hospital. The fewer services members use, the more money the HMO gets to keep. For these programs, a low census is a good sign. In fact, many organizations with capitated contracts have outpatient clinics, and they put health and wellness programs in place to keep patients out of hospital beds and only admit patients when absolutely necessary. Hospitals are then left to figure out creative, innovative ways to provide quality patient care at the lowest cost possible.

IPA

In the IPA model, a group of privately practicing physicians join together to form a coalition that offers managed health organizations a full spectrum of services. These physicians continue to treat patients with third-party payers while serving HMO members. This model is highly controversial, as it raises many ethical questions regarding issues such as the average length of time physicians spend with HMO patients vs. other patients and the number of diagnostic tests physicians request for their HMO patients. These questions arise because in this model, the more resources physicians use, the less they are paid.

PPO

The preferred provider organization (PPO) is a negotiated arrangement between providers and third-party payers. When a physician joins the organization, he or she agrees to abide by the rules and standards within the PPO's reimbursement structure.

The bigger picture

As a financial manager, you should always keep the big picture in mind. For instance, even though you do not have control over the payer mix admitted to your unit, you need to know your hospital's payer mix. The payer mix may differ dramatically depending on your facility's geographic location. For instance, a large urban teaching hospital will likely have more uninsured patients than a small, suburban community hospital. Each patient-care unit is its own business, and as the nurse manager, you are the chief operating officer of that unit. Knowing the payer mix makeup, or how your hospital is reimbursed, helps you understand why LOS is so important and how using fewer resources equates to increased profit for the hospital.

Understanding the flow of revenue cycle in your facility

As nurse manager, you must have a basic understanding of how revenues flow into and out of the hospital. Figure 1.2 shows a typical revenue cycle.

Sample revenue cycle

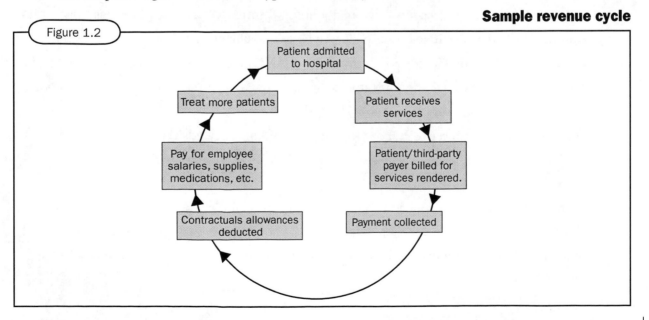

Figure 1.2

- Patient admitted to hospital
- Patient receives services
- Patient/third-party payer billed for services rendered.
- Payment collected
- Contractuals allowances deducted
- Pay for employee salaries, supplies, medications, etc.
- Treat more patients

Hospital hierarchy

In addition to understanding how revenue circulates throughout your hospital, it is also imperative that you know how professional power flows. Power flows are particularly important for nurse managers to know and understand because you deal with and present budgets to the financial experts within your organization. To get a better understanding of the typical financial hierarchy in hospitals, review Figure 1.3.

Financial hierarchy in hospitals

Figure 1.3

The governing board or board of directors is held accountable for the organization's financial performance and therefore has final approval of the budget. Board members are usually local business and community leaders who are not hospital employees. As the governing board, they empower the chief executive officer (CEO) to be responsible for the hospital's management, according to The Joint Commission's (formerly JCAHO) management standard. The CEO, in turn, empowers his or her administrative team to manage the organization's daily operations.

The chief financial officer (CFO) or vice president of finance heads the department and he or she handles all of the hospital's financial operations. CFOs are employees of the hospital.

In the past, the CFO developed the budgets for each unit and presented them to the CNE. The CNE would then present that budget to his or her direct reports (i.e., nursing directors and managers). Today, most CNEs serve at the same level as CFOs and are expected to have the necessary financial and business skills to perform this expanded role. Likewise, nurse managers are now responsible for learning and understanding the tasks related to the financial aspects of their departments—including budget development—for which they are held accountable. In fact, The Joint Commission requires managers to be involved in the budgeting process.

The finance department includes the accounting, payroll, and patient accounting divisions. The finance department manages the financial resources (i.e., cash, investments, and accounts receivable) of the hospital. This department or division is responsible for the following functions:

- Financial planning and auditing
- Accounting services
- Reimbursement and fiscal projects
- Data processing
- Patient financial services

Interdepartmental communication

As nurse manager, hone your skills in communicating effectively with other departments. This is important because departments outside of nursing or outside of the cost center—the cost center being any department that accumulates costs—often affect your unit's business. For example, the nursing unit may be charged for biomedical services performed on unit equipment for preventive maintenance. As nurse manager, you must know the cost and timing of such services so you can keep track of the money in your department's budget.

You must establish strong relationships not only with vendors and other clinical departments but also with the finance department. Engaging the finance department in the actual activities and services of your unit and maintaining healthy relationships with that team enables conversations to flow freely among units, allowing each department to express its needs. Waiting until your formal budget presentation is not a good time to negotiate what your unit needs.

Learning the foreign language of finance

In nursing school, nurses are taught a vocabulary specific to the profession. To the untrained ear, this nursing language can seem confusing. It's the same with finance and accounting professionals: They use only their own terminology to communicate. Learn the language of finance to make your job easier and help you gain the respect of finance personnel.

Figure 1.4 lists some of the financial acronyms and abbreviations commonly used in hospitals.

Glossary of key acronyms and terms

Figure 1.4	
ADC: average daily census	**Patient day:** an admitted patient in a hospital bed at midnight
ALOS: average length of stay	
Assets: liabilities + equity	**PPO:** preferred provider organization
CPUOS: cost per unit of service	**Productive:** actual time worked
Expenses: costs	**Productivity:** output/input
FTE: full-time equivalent	**PTO:** paid time off
Gross revenue: charges	**ROI:** return on investment
HMO: health maintenance organization	**RVU:** relative value unit
HPPD: hours per patient day	**SWB:** salary, wages, and benefits
Liabilities: financial obligations or debt	**UOS:** unit of service
LOS: length of stay	**Volume:** number of patients, tests, visits, procedures, etc.
Nonproductive: nonworked time	

We will discuss each of these terms at length in Chapters 1 and 3.

UOS: A unit of service, or UOS, is the specific item the organization produces and delivers to its customers. For instance, the UOS in nursing departments is typically an admitted patient who is in the hospital bed at midnight. In ancillary departments, such as respiratory therapy, laboratory, and radiology, UOSs may be the number of treatments, tests, or doses given to a patient. As nurse manager, you may be responsible for managing both inpatient and outpatient areas as well as supervising an ancillary service. Therefore, it's important that you know how UOSs are measured. In the nursing example, the admitted patient in a hospital bed at midnight (the UOS) is the measurement. In ancillary departments, each procedure, depending on its complexity, is assigned a relative value unit (RVU). For instance, with respiratory therapy, setting up oxygen may count as one RVU, whereas checking a ventilator may be allocated three RVUs.

ADC: The average daily census (ADC) is the number of admitted patients (inpatients) on any given day. However, depending on a hospital's operation, this may include observation patients. To determine the ADC you divide the number of patient days in a given period by the number of days in that period. For example, in a nursing unit that is budgeted to use 7,500 UOSs per year, divide the number of UOSs by the number of days in a year (365) to find out the ADC. So, 7,500 ÷ 365 = 20.55 average patients on the unit per day.

ALOS: The average length of stay (ALOS) is the average number of days patients spent in the hospital. Find this by dividing the number of patient days in a given period by the number of discharges in that period. For example, if your unit experienced 180 patient days and 50 discharges in one week, your ALOS would be 3.6 (180 ÷ 50 = 3.6). Therefore, your patients stay in your unit for an average of 3.6 days.

CPUOS: The cost per UOS (CPUOS) is defined as the total cost of salaries divided by the units of service. You can use this financial measurement for any expense that occurs on the unit, but it is primarily used for salaries. To calculate salary CPUOS, take the total worked hours by staff and multiply it by the hourly rate. Then divide that amount by the UOS for that unit. For example, if the total salaries were $102,000 and the UOS were 660 for the month, then the total CPUOS would be $154.55 ($102,000 ÷ 660 = $154.55) for worked hours. You can also calculate the total CPUOS by adding in the non-worked hours. The breakdown of these two categories will be explained in a later chapter.

FTE: A full-time equivalent (FTE) is the equivalent of one full-time employee working for one year. This is generally calculated as 40 hours per week for 52 weeks or as a total of 2,080 paid hours per year. This includes both productive and nonproductive (i.e., vacation, sick, holiday) time. For example, two employees working half-time for one year equal one FTE. To calculate FTE, multiply the length of the shifts by the number of days worked. Then divide the total by 40 hours, the number of hours worked by a full-time employee. For example, if a nurse works three eight-hour shifts per week, the FTE would be 0.6 (8 X 3 = 24 ÷ 40 = 0.6).

Volume: The term "volume" refers to the number of patients admitted or in the bed at midnight; the number of treatments, tests, or procedures patients undergo, and the number of meals served, etc.

Productivity: Simply stated, productivity is output divided by input. Productivity rates measure the input required for a unit of output. When put into practice in hospitals, productivity is the number of staff who were used—either by hours or dollars—divided by the number of

UOS used (i.e., midnight census on inpatient units). By comparing the actual staffing hours with the staffing hours required—while taking patient acuity levels into consideration—you can determine the standard productivity measure used in hospitals.

These terms and acronyms are some of the basics used in hospitals today. Incorporate them into your daily vocabulary. Understanding these terms—and how they fit into the big picture—will enable you to be more efficient and productive in your role.

BONUS TOOLS

You will find a financial terminology cheat sheet and the top five survival skills every manager should know on the CD-ROM accompanying this book.

'Talking the talk' scenario

Review the following scenario and think about the correct and incorrect ways to handle the situation:

New nurse manager Carey Carrington runs a busy telemetry unit. The unit is particularly difficult to manage because it has 85 staff members and an ADC of 26 patients. Patients are constantly transferring in and out of the unit.

Each week, Carey's productivity report reflects a large variance toward the beginning of the week, but her unit's midnight census has remained consistent. When reviewing the previous month's staffing reports and admission/discharge/transfer data, Carey found that an average of 20 new patients flowed through the unit during the same 12-hour period every Tuesday. She discovered that the patients were not captured in the midnight census.

Carey is scheduled to meet with her supervisor in the morning. What should she say?

Incorrect: "Tuesdays are really busy on the unit; we are always short-staffed and some of my nurses are threatening to quit. I need to hire another nurse. Can you please sign this hiring form so I can take it to HR and begin advertising?"

Correct: "After collecting data and observing the unit for the past 90 days, I have found that as a result of the cardiac catheterization lab scheduling, we take on an average of five extra cases each Tuesday. Along with the added cases, the intensive care unit census is running to capacity. Therefore, we have turned over an average of 20 patients every Tuesday for the past three months. And although our productivity reports show an ADC of 26, we are actually caring for 46 patients over the course of the day.

"I would like approval to increase staffing on Tuesdays, and I will modify the schedule accordingly. Currently, we are reducing staff on Fridays because of the lowered census, which will help maintain the overall budgeted HPPD. I will explain the variances each month on the variance report. I anticipate the overall CPUOS to remain the same."

Chapter

FINANCIAL MANAGEMENT AND
BASIC COST ACCOUNTING

Learning objectives

After reading this chapter, the learner will be able to:

- Identify the components of a financial statement
- Explain the differences between a balance sheet and income and departmental expenditures

Financial reports

Various financial reports or statements indicate an organization's financial health, and it is imperative that you are able to read, analyze, and understand them. Have no fear: Understanding the terminology and practices related to finance management and accounting is a skill that you will pick up through practice. This chapter will introduce you to the basic principles of accounting and show you how to read and recognize financial statements.

When reviewing the sample statements throughout this chapter, be aware that your organization's statements and line items (i.e., purchased services) may read differently. Find out exactly which services/fees fall under the line items in your organization's financial statements.

Hospital accounting

Every hospital or healthcare organization has a formal accounting system to track its finances. Whether you work at a for- or not-for-profit organization, the accounting terms, functions, and rules are basically the same. These rules are known as generally accepted accounting principles (GAAP). GAAP were established by the Financial Accounting Standards Board (FASB)—an organization that determines the standards for financial accounting and reporting.

The following financial equation is widely practiced in business:

Assets = Liabilities + owner's equity

Assets are any tangible or intangible resources or property owned by the organization. Examples of assets include cash, buildings, equipment, and inventory.

Liabilities are the financial obligations or debts owed to others by the organization. Examples of liabilities include accounts payable, wages payable, and bonds payable.

Owner's equity, or net worth, refers to the assets an organization or its owners possess.

Financial statements

Balance sheet

The most significant financial statement in a hospital is the balance sheet. The balance sheet is a document that outlines the organization's assets, liabilities, and net worth at a particular point in time. Its contents change daily. It acts as a snapshot of the hospital's financial state, showing what the hospital owes and owns. It affects the organization's credit line, which affects its ability to build, borrow, or grow.

The creation of net worth for not-for-profit hospitals occurs when there is an excess of revenues over expenses. When the same happens in for-profit institutions, the excess is referred to as profit. The profit is then divided among the shareholders, and any leftover money is reinvested into the facility for such projects as adding additional services or constructing a new wing.

When looking at a balance sheet for the first time, it is easy to become frustrated and overwhelmed. Just remember that once you view a few of them, you will learn exactly what to look for, and it will be a piece of cake. To help you read and understand a balance sheet, we dissect the sample balance sheet in Figure 2.1.

Sample balance sheet

Figure 2.1

	2008	2007
Current assets		
Cash and investments		
	$500,000	$750,000
Accounts receivable		
Patient revenues	$5,000,000	$3,400,000
Less:		
Bad debts	$300,000	$150,000
Charitable allowances	$50,000	$50,000
Contractual allowances	$450,000	$375,000
Inventory	$225,000	$199,000
TOTAL CURRENT ASSETS	$4,925,000	$3,774,000
Fixed assets		
Land	$3,530,000	$3,530,000
Buildings, (plant)	$12,500,000	$12,000,000
Equipment	$4,500,000	$3,500,000
Construction in progress	$1,500,000	$800,000
Total fixed assets	$22,030,000	$19,830,000
Less: Depreciation	$3,800,000	$2,700,000
NET FIXED ASSETS	$18,230,000	$17,130,000
TOTAL ASSETS	$23,155,000	$20,904,000
Current liabilities		
Accounts payable	$2,500,000	$1,500,000
Accrued compensation and benefits	$250,000	$350,000
Accrued liabilities (interest, physician payments)	$100,000	$90,000
Current portion of long-term debt	$100,000	$50,000
TOTAL CURRENT LIABILITIES	$2,950,000	$1,990,000
Long-term liabilities		
Bonds payable	$15,000,000	$14,000,000
Mortgage payable	$500,000	$650,000
NET WORTH	**$4,705,000**	**$4,255,000**

TIP

Sometimes, the last group of 000s is dropped from numbers, meaning all the numbers have been rounded to the nearest thousand dollars. This is done on balance sheets and income statements to conserve space and make the report easier to read.

First, it's important to know that items on the balance sheet are placed in order of liquidity, from the most liquid to the least liquid. This means those assets that can be turned into cash quickly, also known as liquid assets, are positioned at the top of the balance sheet to show financial stability.

Current assets

Let's review the first section, current assets (Figure 2.2), from the balance sheet.

Current assets

Figure 2.2

	2008	2007
Current assets		
Cash and investments		
	$500,000	$750,000
Accounts receivable		
Patient revenues	$5,000,000	$3,400,000
Less:		
Bad debts	300,000	150,000
Charitable allowances	50,000	50,000
Contractual allowances	450,000	375,000
Inventory	225,000	199,000
TOTAL CURRENT ASSETS	**$4,925,000**	**$3,774,000**

Cash is the most liquid asset and is always listed first. Cash constitutes all cash on hand/in checking or savings accounts. This also includes short-term certificates of deposit.

Marketable securities, which are short-term **investments** such as stocks and bonds, usually are listed next. If the intent of the organization is to sell these stocks or bonds within one year, they are listed under current assets. However, if the organization plans to hold onto them for more than a year, such investments are listed under the fixed assets section.

Accounts receivable (AR) refers to the assets that the patient or insurer is responsible for paying. Invoices are sent to patients or insurers charging them for services incurred, and payment is expected within 30 days. Therefore, on the balance sheet, AR represents the amount of money owed to the hospital. Finance departments often report their aging accounts to the chief executive officer. These aging accounts are often categorized by days, such as zero to 30, 30–45, 45–60, and over 60. By referring to the age of the account, the hospital can then determine when to write off these uncollected accounts as bad debt, meaning that the hospital will not recoup the money.

Patient revenues are all of the charges made to insurance companies and patients for outstanding payments for the time period covered on the report.

Charitable allowances are the amount of money the hospital budgets for free care. Most organizations provide a certain amount of free care to patients that will never be able to pay for services. These charges are eventually written off.

Although a hospital's goal is to collect all the monies owed to it, not all AR are collectable. Because of contractual allowances and bad debt, hospitals never receive 100% of what they bill. The term **contractual allowances** refers to the difference between the amount the hospital bills Medicare, Medicaid, or other third-party payers and the amount the hospital receives from them.

Inventory represents all of the on-hand stock/supplies the organization owns to provide services in the future. Some examples of inventory include linens, medications, tubing, and intravenous (IV) kits. Items in the inventory category are considered current assets because, if necessary, they can easily be converted into cash.

Fixed assets

Fixed assets are long-term assets that include property, equipment, land, and buildings. Let's review the second section, fixed assets (Figure 2.3), from the balance sheet.

Figure 2.3		Fixed assets
	2008	**2007**
Fixed assets		
Land	$3,530,000	$3,530,000
Buildings, (plant)	$12,500,000	$12,000,000
Equipment	$4,500,000	$3,500,000
Construction in progress	$1,500,000	$800,000
Total fixed assets	$22,030,000	$19,830,000
Less: Depreciation	$3,800,000	$2,700,000
NET FIXED ASSETS	**$18,230,000**	**$17,130,000**

Land is property owned by the organization. It includes the land that the hospital and other medical office buildings (MOB) reside on as well as land obtained for future development or use.

Buildings include the hospital itself, MOBs, clinics, pharmacies, laboratories, and nursing homes owned by the organization.

Equipment is materials or devices used within the hospital or its other facilities. Examples of equipment include computer tomography scanners, magnetic resonance imaging machines, and surgical and cardiac catheterization laboratory equipment.

Construction in progress is exactly as it sounds. It includes all structural additions or renovations being made to buildings, wings, or units owned by the organization.

Depreciation refers to the loss of value property undergoes when it ages or becomes obsolete. In other words, when fixed assets lose their value, they lose their effectiveness for the organization. Therefore, it is important to take eventual depreciation into consideration when purchasing or appraising the value of a fixed asset. However, know that calculating depreciation is typically a task for the finance department.

Net fixed assets is determined by subtracting depreciation from the total fixed assets. Use the numbers for 2007 in Figure 2.3 to calculate the sample hospital's net fixed assets: ($22,030,000 – $3,800,000 = $18,230,000 net fixed assets).

Current liabilities

Toward the bottom of the balance sheet, you will find liabilities and owner's equity. Liabilities on the sheet are divided into current and long-term. **Current liabilities** are the organization's obligations or debts that it expects to pay off within one year. **Long-term liabilities**, or long-term debts, are paid after a one-year period.

Let's review the current liabilities section (Figure 2.4) from the balance sheet.

Figure 2.4		**Current liabilities**
	2008	**2007**
Current liabilities		
Accounts payable	$2,500,000	$1,500,000
Accrued compensation and benefits	$250,000	$350,000
Accrued liabilities (interest, physician payments)	$100,000	$90,000
Current portion of long-term debt	$100,000	$50,000
TOTAL CURRENT LIABILITIES	**$2,950,000**	**$1,990,000**

Accounts payable refers to unpaid balances with suppliers (i.e., medical and nonmedical supplies bought from pharmaceutical companies with credit).

Accrued compensation and benefits, or accrued wages payable, are salaries and benefits to be paid to employees. These accrue during the pay period cycle.

Other current liabilities

Notes payable are another form of current liabilities. They are short-term promissory notes owed to the bank or lending agency that must be repaid within one year. **Taxes payable** are also current liabilities and are taxes owed to the state, federal, or local government. For for-profit organizations, this means paying real estate, sales, and income taxes. Not-for-profit organizations do not have to pay taxes and are thus tax exempt. However, they must still pay taxes on unemployment benefits and workers' compensation. Some balance sheets also have a line item called "deferred revenues." The term **deferred revenues** refers to payment the hospital has received from an outside agency or employer for services that the hospital has not yet given. For example, the hospital is contracted to give out flu shots to an organization, but until the shots are administered, the revenue is a liability.

Long-term liabilities

Long-term liabilities are debts that the organization plans to pay off at least 12 months after the date on the balance sheet. In other words, they are debts that the organization plans to settle after the 12-month payoff period allotted for current liabilities. Examples of long-term care liabilities include bonds payable and mortgage costs.

Let's review the long-term liabilities section (Figure 2.5) from the balance sheet.

Long-term liabilities

Figure 2.5	2008	2007
Long-term liabilities		
Bonds payable	$15,000,000	$14,000,000
Mortgage payable	500,000	650,000
Net worth	**$4,705,000**	**$4,255,000**

Bonds payable are bonds that the organization issues and therefore must make scheduled payments toward, with interest that it pays to the bondholder for the use of the bondholder's money. Bonds are written promises made by organizations, or issuers, to investors stating that money borrowed will be paid back with interest on a chosen date. Typically, bonds are paid back in five or more years. Hospitals issue or "float" bonds for various reasons (i.e., for additional capital to construct a building).

Mortgage payable is the monthly mortgage(s) the organization must pay, with interest, for a time period greater than 12 months.

Net worth

Net worth is the value or worth of an organization after paying off all of its debts or liabilities. Remember: assets – liabilities = net worth.

Depending whether the organization is for-profit or not-for-profit, names for the net worth line on the balance sheet may vary. For instance, when dealing with a for-profit organization, this line is usually called either net worth or fund balance. It may also be called owner's or shareholder's equity. On a not-for-profit's balance sheet, however, you will see it called fund balance.

The net worth line usually includes detailed information, which may include stockholder's equity and "retained earnings." **Retained earnings** are earnings the organization sets aside for future construction or expansion projects. These earnings represent the profit that is not distributed to shareholders or owners in the form of a dividend.

Income statement

The income statement is the second major financial statement for the organization. Also referred to as the profit and loss or operating statements, income statements summarize organizational and departmental revenue and expense activities. You are responsible for understanding the departmental income statement. However, like with everything in healthcare, it's important to look at the larger picture to help yourself understand the smaller one.

Let's begin our breakdown of an income statement by looking at Figure 2.6.

Sample income statement

Figure 2.6

(Profit and loss)
($000s omitted)

	2008	2007
Gross patient revenues		
Routine services	$23,000	$21,500
Inpatient ancillary	$22,000	$18,500
Outpatient ancillary	$11,000	$6,000
Other revenue	$500	$150
TOTAL GROSS REVENUE	$56,500	$46,150
Deductions from revenue		
Bad debt	$3,000	$2,500
Governmental allowances	$12,500	$8,500
Insurance contracts	$5,000	$3,100
Charitable allowances	$500	$1,000
TOTAL DEDUCTIONS	$21,000	$14,100
NET REVENUE FROM PATIENTS	$35,500	$32,050
Operating expenses		
Salaries	$14,800	$13,500
Benefits	$2,400	$2,200
Supplies	$4,850	$3,950
Medical fees	$1,300	$1,200
Purchased services	$5,000	$3,800
Maintenance	$1,800	$1,600
Professional liability	$400	$300
Other	$800	$400
Depreciation	$1,900	$1,700
Financing costs	$1,400	$1,300
TOTAL OPERATING EXPENSES	$34,650	$29,950
NET (Pre-tax) INCOME FROM OPERATIONS	$850	$2,100
PERCENT OF NET REVENUE (MARGIN)	2.4%	6.5%

The purpose of an income statement is to see how effectively money flows into and out of an organization by comparing its income and expenses for a particular month or year with the figures for the same time period one year prior.

Gross patient revenues

Following GAAP principles, revenues from patients—the largest revenue source—are listed first on the income statement. Expenses are listed later in the statement as they will be subtracted from the revenues. Let's review Figure 2.7, which shows gross patient revenues from the sample income statement.

Gross patient revenues

Figure 2.7

(Note: $000s omitted)

	2008	2007
Gross patient revenues		
Routine services	$23,000	$21,500
Inpatient ancillary	$22,000	$18,500
Outpatient ancillary	$11,000	$6,000
Other revenue	$500	$150
TOTAL GROSS REVENUE	**$56,500**	**$46,150**

Gross patient revenue is all charges for services that the hospital provided. Typically, such revenue is broken down into the following categories:

- **Routine services,** which include room charges, medication, food, etc.

- **Inpatient ancillary,** which includes respiratory therapy treatments, x-rays, physical therapy, etc.

- **Outpatient ancillary,** which includes short-stay surgical patients, therapy, etc.

- **Other revenue,** which refers to sales from the gift shop, cafeteria, etc.

Deductions from revenue

Let's break down deductions from revenue, shown in Figure 2.8.

Deductions from revenue

Figure 2.8

(Note: $000s omitted)

	2008	2007
Deductions from revenue		
Bad debt	$3,000	$2,500
Governmental allowances	$12,500	$8,500
Insurance contracts	$5,000	$3,100
Charitable allowances	$500	$1,000
TOTAL DEDUCTIONS	**$21,000**	**$14,100**

Deduction from revenue is the amount subtracted from the actual charges. Typically, such deductions include the following categories:

- **Bad debt,** which includes charges that will not be paid by patients who were expected to pay

- **Governmental allowances,** which include the Medicare or Medicaid discounts from full charges

- **Insurance contracts,** which are contracts, such as with health maintenance organizations or other providers' discounts, that have been negotiated and agreed to by the hospital

- **Charitable allowances,** or free care, which include those charges that the hospital won't be reimbursed for by patients who were not expected to pay

Contractual allowances are another deduction from revenue category you might find on an income statement. This category includes Medicare, Medicaid, and other third-party payer discounts and shows the deductions from revenue v. the gross revenue.

Net revenue from patients

Net revenue from patients is calculated by subtracting the total deductions from the total gross revenue. Use the amounts from 2007 in the sample hospital's income statement in Figure 2.6 to calculate net revenue from patients ($56,500 – $21,000 = $35,500 net revenue from patients).

Operating expenses

Operating expenses are all of the costs necessary for running an organization. Let's review Figure 2.9, which shows the operating expenses from the income statement.

Operating expenses

Figure 2.9		

(Note: $000s omitted)

	2008	**2007**
Operating expenses		
Salaries	$14,800	$13,500
Benefits	$2,400	$2,200
Supplies	$4,850	$3,950
Medical fees	$1,300	$1,200
Purchased services	$5,000	$3,800
Maintenance	$1,800	$1,600
Professional liability	$400	$300
Other	$800	$400
Depreciation	$1,900	$1,700
Financing costs	$1,400	$1,300
TOTAL OPERATING EXPENSES	**$34,650**	**$29,950**

Salaries and wages are the largest expense for a hospital. This expense can be broken down further into direct and indirect salaries. Indirect salaries are given to caregivers who do not work directly with patients, such as management, secretarial, and administration. Direct and indirect costs are discussed further in Chapter 3.

Benefits for employees are another operating expense. Some benefits include medical, dental, and vision insurance and holiday, vacation, and sick pay. These and other benefits usually amount to between 25%–35% of wages, depending on the organization.

Supplies generally include medical items, such as 4x4s, sutures, and catheters as well as non-medical supplies such as fax paper, pens, pencils, forms, etc.

Medical fees are those paid to physicians by a hospital for the work they do within the organization—for example, the monthly stipend a physician is paid for acting as the medical director of a particular service.

Purchased services include fees for traveling nurses, outside contract labor, or entire outsourced services, such as housekeeping or nutritional services. Purchased services are a line on the income statement that you'll become familiar with, because you may use this section to pay for some nursing salaries.

Maintenance expenses are those related to the upkeep and ongoing preventive care of the organization and its equipment.

Professional liability refers to the liability insurance premiums the hospital must pay to cover potential lawsuits.

Other expenses are those that do not fit into the above categories. They might include cab fare for indigent patients, flowers for a holiday party, and other such expenses.

Depreciation, as previously discussed, is the loss in value the organization anticipates for its buildings or equipment. Although it's good to understand depreciation, as nurse manager, you are not responsible for calculating it—the finance department is.

Financing costs refer to the expenses an organization pays toward money it has borrowed to replace or improve the hospital or its equipment.

Net income from operations

Net income from operations is calculated by subtracting the total operating expenses from the net revenues received from patients. Use the figures for 2003 on the sample statement to calculate the net income from operations in Figure 2.6 ($35,500 – $34,650 = $850 net income for operations).

The **percent of net revenue,** also known as the operating margin or bottom line, is determined by dividing the net income from operations by the net revenue from patients. Use the figures from 2007 to calculate the percent of net revenue ($850 ÷ $35,500 = 0.024, or 2.4%).

A healthy bottom line, also called the "margin," is above zero. If the margin is below that, it indicates the hospital is losing money. Most hospitals like the margin to be between 3%–8%.

Departmental income statement

The departmental income statement goes by many aliases, including cost center report, profit and loss statement, and trend report. For the purposes of this book, the departmental income statement is referred to as the cost center report.

You should receive these reports monthly and for multiple cost centers. A cost center is a unit of the hospital that accumulates costs. Such departments have distinct budgets for revenue and expenses as well as managers assigned to control them. Each department is identified and tracked through these designated numbers. Many times, units are split into two or more cost centers for more effective management. For example, in the obstetrics department, labor and delivery may have a single, separate cost center from post-partum and nursery, even though one manager is responsible for all three areas. Depending on the organization's size, cost centers may be rolled up into one report. Often, each division will produce reports for several cost centers.

The financial data on cost center reports are divided into department, division, or total hospital categories. Each manager receives his or her own cost center report, whereas directors receive reports containing information for all their cost centers. The hospital report lists all the cost centers. For health systems with numerous hospitals, regional and national reports may be compiled. As nurse manager, you will not receive all of these reports. However, if you are interested in seeing them, ask your supervisor or finance department for access to them.

The difference between the departmental cost center reports and income statements for the entire hospital is that department reports thoroughly break down revenue and expenses by units and cost centers to help managers keep a close eye on the money going into and out of their units.

From the cost center report, you can track the revenue that came into the unit and the unit's operating costs for a chosen month and compare the operating costs for one month to those for the same month one year prior. Another benefit of the cost center report is the cost per unit of service (CPUOS) breakdown, which divides both salaries and hours by the total units of service (UOS) used during a specific time period. Negative variances are noted in parentheses. As with the organizational income statement, revenue is at the top followed by expenses and a breakdown of CPUOS and hours per patient day (HPPD).

Let's review the sample cost center report in Figure 2.10. This sample depicts a nursing unit (telemetry), for which the unit of service is a patient day. For ancillary departments, the UOS is the specific item that department produces and delivers.

Sample cost center report

Figure 2.10

Department: Telemetry   **Manager:** Susie Smith
Cost center: 6150
Period ending: June 30, 2008

Current month					Description	Year to date				
Actual	**Budget**	**Variance**	**Var %**	**Prior yr**	**Revenue**	**Actual**	**Budget**	**Variance**	**Var %**	**Prior yr**
1,400,000 0	1,040,000 0	360,000 0	35%	915,000 0	Inpatient revenue	15,253,126 0	12,062,013 0	3,191,113 0	26%	13,748,936
					Outpatient revenue				100%	250
1,400,000	1,040,000	360,000	35%	915,000	**Total revenue**	15,253,126	12,062,013	3,191,113	26%	13,749,186
					Expenses					
222,156	191,952	(30, 204)	(16%)	198,554	Salaries and wages	2,469,073	2,229,607	(39,466)	(11%)	2,359,006
105,005	90,000	(15,005)	(17%)	101,775	Benefits	302,404	313,963	11,559	4%	307,449
85,000	60,000	(25,000)	(42%)	54,332	Professional fees	1,118,881	728,346	390,535	(54%)	663,951
150	200	50	25%	188	Purchased services	2,338	1,150	1,188	(103%)	1,872
13,222	12,654	(568)	(5%)	11,952	Supplies	155,409	162,654	(7,245)	45%	145,739
1,500	600	(900)	(250%)	720	Other	6,050	1,942	4,108	(212%)	2,378
8,263	8,152	(111)	(1%)	8,152	Depreciation	105,968	106,942	974	(.9%)	106,942
435,296	363,558	(71,738)	(20%)	388,761	Total Expenses	4,160,123	3,544,604	615,519	(17%)	3,644,795
Actual	**Budget**	**Variance**	**Var %**	**Prior yr**	**Statistics**	**Actual**	**Budget**	**Variance**	**Var %**	**Prior yr**
625	605	20	3%	645	UOS	8,224	7,642	582	8%	7,888
8,362	7,528	(834)	(11%)	8,109	Productive hours	107,651	93,239	14,412	(15%)	95,386
998	1,012	14	1%	975	Nonprod. hours	10,992	11,377	(385)	3%	11,445
9,360	8,540	(820)	(10%)	9,084	Total paid hours	118,643	104,616	14,027	(13%)	110,398
13.38	12.44	0.94	(7%)	12.57	Productive hours/ UOS	13.08	12.20	0.88	(7%)	12.09
14.98	14.12	0.86	(6%)	14.08	Paid hours/UOS	14.43	13.68	0.75	(5%)	13.99

Key: Prod hours/UOS = Total productive hours divided by UOS
        Paid hours/UOS = Total paid hours divided by UOS
        Variance = Actual minus budget
        Variance % = Variance divided by budget
        Prior year = Last year, same month, actual
        (+) = Favorable expense variance
        (–) = Unfavorable expense variance

Revenue

When analyzing the cost center report in Figure 2.10, look at the revenue section. You will notice that more charges were made during June ($1,400,000) than were allowed for in the budget ($1,040,000). Remember: The total revenue constitutes charges before contractual allowances are made. In a given hospital, this number may be either gross revenue or net revenue, depending on whether the contractual allowances have been deducted at the unit level.

Although some hospitals use a contractual allowances line on the departmental report to show net revenue, the sample cost center report in Figure 2.10 only shows gross revenue. As you can see, the majority of revenue for this cost center comes from inpatient services, or **inpatient revenue,** with a small amount ($500) coming from **outpatient services,** or outpatient revenue, collected at some point during the year.

As nurse manager, you do not have control over inpatient revenue; therefore, focus on the expenses in the report. In Chapter 3, we will further discuss what managers control in their budget. For now, let's focus on expenses.

Expenses

Expenses are an important section in the cost center report that you need to understand. This is because expenses are a large part of what you are responsible for, such as staff's salaries and wages, which constitute the largest expenses. Cost center reports typically are broken down into the following job categories:

- Registered nurse (RN)
- Licensed Practical/Vocational Nurse (LPN/LVN)
- Clerical
- Physical Therapist
- Respiratory Therapist
- Technician
- Pharmacist
- Assistant
- Other

However, in Figure 2.10, salaries are lumped into one.

TIP

If your cost center report does not have staff's salaries and wages broken down by job type, ask your finance department to do so.

According to the sample cost center report, actual salaries and wages were at $222,156, which is $30,204 over budget. That means that the unit ended up using more or more expensive staff than were budgeted for. You must explain this negative variance of $30,204 to the administrative department. There are tools and tips to help you analyze and communicate your budget with others in Chapter 4.

Benefits were also over budget in June. According to the sample report, benefits include vacation and sick time, holidays, and education, such as conferences staff attended or meetings that were held. It also includes paid days off or earned time off.

You must know exactly how your hospital defines "benefits" because the term is often broken down further into vacation, holiday, sick, workers' compensation, education, training, etc. Some hospitals might lump this all together. If that is the case, ask the finance department for source documents so you can complete your analysis.

You also may see the benefits item referred to as nonproductive on some cost center reports. Although you will have little to do with this item, keep track of the amount of vacation and sick time used. Sick leave also may include workers' compensation payments, so check with the finance department for a clear definition of what constitutes sick leave.

TIP

Keep an eye out for the things that negatively affect benefits' variance, such as extended sick leaves, long-term employees with high amounts of unused vacation time transferring to your cost center, and increases in mandatory education that were not budgeted for (i.e., new equipment, in-services, new Joint Commission regulations, etc.).

For many organizations, **professional fees** are those paid out by the organization to obtain staff. Professional fees include those for medical/physician, outside agency RNs or LPNs, and travel nurses brought in for high census days. Salaries of agency staff employed with the hospital are included in regular salaries. Sometimes expenses for outside temporary staff are found under the "purchased services" category. In the sample cost center report, all outside temporary staff are found under the professional fees category. In hospitals that use a high number of travel nurses, depending on the mix of travel nurses and regular staff, it is possible that a unit would come in under budget for regular salaries and over budget for purchased services.

Purchased services may include travelers, repairs, maintenance, catering, and any outside contracts (i.e., the copy machine) or other purchased services that may be allocated to your cost center. For example, if your organization uses an outside agency to provide housekeeping, this expense may be charged to each individual cost center.

Supplies consist of IV solutions, pharmaceuticals, cleaning supplies, medical supplies, sutures, scrubs, office supplies, and minor equipment (e.g., otoscopes, thermometers). As with the other categories, supplies can be broken down if you would like more detailed information. In fact, the report can go into such detail that, if requested, you could find out the exact number of IV tubings or O2 tubings used on your unit.

Other expenses include items such as outside travel (e.g., sending nurses to outside conferences), dues and subscriptions (e.g., Physicians' Desk Reference and nursing journals), and rent/lease charges for equipment (e.g., IV pumps, telemetry/ventilators).

Depreciation, as you can imagine, is listed as an expense. If the unit has large equipment that will lose value, it is listed in this category.

Total expenses

All monthly expenses are added together to determine operating expenses. The total is then compared to the current month's budget and the total for the same month of the prior year.

Statistics

The statistics, broken down by UOS, typically follow expenses on the cost center report. The total UOS, such as patients who are admitted and are in a bed at midnight, are added for the month, and the total is listed.

Productive hours refer to the actual hours worked. As expected, the actual productive hours (8,362 hours) were 834 hours higher than were budgeted (7,528 hours) because the unit cared for more patients than planned. However, when divided by the UOS, you can see that the **productive hours per UOS** (13.38), or HPPD, were higher than budgeted. You must defend this variance to the members of the administrative department. However, you cannot do so by telling them that your hours and dollars are higher because of higher volume, as that argument would not match the figures. The increase in hours (834 hours) was not proportionate to the increase in UOS (20).

The cost center report is one of the most important reports, as it provides a detailed summary of all of the financial activity on the unit. Become familiar with this report. It is imperative to your success.

BONUS TOOLS

You will find cheat sheets of key income statement terms and key balance sheet terms every manager should know on the CD-ROM accompanying this book.

Chapter 3

BUILDING A BUDGET

Learning objectives

After reading this chapter, the learner will be able to:

- Describe the process of budgeting for staff, supplies, equipment, and capital expenditures
- Identify the process to construct a budget

The budget cycle

A budget is a financial plan that outlines the resources an entity foresees using for a particular time period. The master budget encompasses all the departmental budgets. Based on the organization's strategic goals and vision, the master budget is the actual statement of projected revenues and expenditures for the entire hospital.

Developing a budget is an ongoing process. See the budget cycle in Figure 3.1 on the following page to better understand the order and process of the budget cycle.

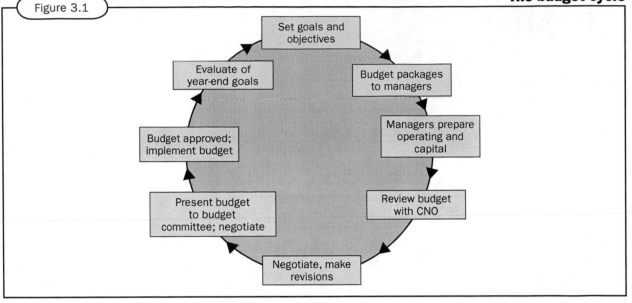

The budget cycle

Figure 3.1

The budget cycle typically involves an environmental assessment that looks at trends in healthcare and in the hospital as well as its competition. Once such assessments are made, the hospital's goals and objectives are evaluated to determine whether any changes must be made. If changes must be made, the unit's goals are set based on the prior year's performance, trends in the marketplace, and assumptions about the future.

The organization's operational objectives are developed and approved by the administrative department. It is at this point that the formal budget packages—including instructions, projected units of service (UOS), and revenue for the unit—are put together and distributed to department managers. Expect to receive such a package approximately four to six months before the budget is due.

Next, you will prepare your unit budget. At this point, negotiations between the nurse manager and the chief nurse executive (CNE) or chief nursing officer (CNO), as well as any other departments, occur. Once the CNE approves your budget, you present it to the appropriate group(s), which usually consist of administration and the chief financial officer (CFO). The CFO will likely have questions the manager needs to address. Following the meeting with administration and the CFO, you must make the necessary adjustments to your budget. If there is an opportunity to re-present or appeal the budget, this is the time to do so. The budget is then approved, stamped, sealed, and ready to be implemented.

Finally, at the year's end, it is time to evaluate the annual budget. After doing so, you can determine what needs to be modified for next year's budget. Do this by tracking and trending activities and numbers throughout the year to develop a fair and reasonable budget for the following year.

In many hospitals, the finance department and administration work together to develop a budget calendar. This calendar is distributed to all managers and helps keep everyone on the same page with their budgeting tasks for the upcoming year.

BONUS TOOLS

 To review a sample budget calendar, look in the Chapter 3 folder on this book's accompanying CD-ROM.

At the end of the budget cycle, the hospital will create an operating budget that it must present to and get approved by the board of directors. For this presentation, all departmental budgets are rolled into one master budget. (The budget presentation is discussed in depth in Chapter 4.)

Controllable and uncontrollable expenses

You are responsible for managing the activities of your unit; therefore, you must know what you have control over. Typically, you control most of the activities on your unit that contribute to the budget. Such activities include staffing, skill mix, education, staff meetings, and orientation length. At the end of each month, you must explain to your supervisor any discrepancies in the numbers you budgeted. Internal accounting reports are usually given to managers. Such reports show the difference between the expected performance planned in the budget and the actual results.

Your responsibilities are as follows:

1. Controllable expenses

- Staffing
- Supplies

2. Uncontrollable expenses

- Revenue
- Patients' acuity levels and unit activity levels
- Types of benefits

Types of budgets

There are many types of budgets that you may be responsible for or for which you will make contributions.

Revenue budget

You may not be required to calculate revenue for your unit budget, especially if you are in an inpatient setting. You should, however, understand the association of revenue with nursing care, but the finance department controls the charges (i.e., room charges) made to the patients on your unit. For managers who run a unit with multiple levels of care (i.e., medical-surgical and telemetry), the patient room charge is based on the level of care the patient receives on your unit. The level of care is typically based on staffing requirements or patient acuity levels. If a patient qualifies as high acuity, the hospital can charge more for his or her care.

Outpatient areas typically have different reimbursement rates than inpatient areas. Therefore, managers who run outpatient areas, such as a clinic, emergency department, respiratory therapy, pharmacy, or other ancillary areas, may be required to calculate revenue for your budget.

Figure 3.2 depicts how the budgeted revenue is calculated for a unit with a UOS of 7,500 for the year.

| Figure 3.2 | **Sample budgeted revenue for med-surg/telemetry unit** |

(Unit with 26 bed capacity)

Budgeted UOS X room charge = budgeted revenue

Level 1 patients (medical-surgical)   4,000 x $700 = $2,800,000
Level 2 patients (telemetry)   3,500 x $900 = $3,150,000
Total budgeted revenue   **$5,950,000**

53% of all patients projected for next year will be Level 1 medical-surgical
(4,000 ÷ 7,500 = 0.53 or 53%)
47% of all patients projected for next year will be Level 2 telemetry
(3,500 ÷ 7,500 = 0.47 or 47%)

These percentages are determined by using historical data, trends in the market, and other contributing factors, such as insurance contracts and physician practice patterns.

Expense budget

Managers are typically involved in developing two types of budgets: operating and capital. The operating budget entails the unit's day-to-day plan for revenue and expenses. Most nursing units generate expenses, which might include the following:

1. Personnel expenses

   - Wages
   - Salaries
   - Benefits
   - Overtime
   - Orientation
   - Education

2. Other expenses

   - Supplies (medical and nonmedical)
   - Minor equipment
   - Linen
   - Purchased services
   - Maintenance

- Food
- Interdepartmental transfers

As you can see, expenses are broken down into two components: personnel and other expenses. Revenue budgets, such as physical therapy or radiology departments, are broken into inpatient and outpatient revenue.

Personnel budget

The finance department or your supervisor will determine the projected budgeted revenue for your unit, and then expenses must be calculated. As mentioned earlier, the biggest expense in the nursing department—and the hospital—is staff salaries. In fact, salaries often account for up to 75% of department and hospital budgets. The personnel budget determines how much staff is needed to operate the unit 24 hours a day, 365 days a year.

Budgeted staff in nursing includes the following, and may include additional staff at your facility:

- Nurse manager
- Charge nurses
- Registered nurses (RN)
- Licensed practical nurses (LPN)
- Nursing assistants (NA)
- Monitor technicians
- Orderlies
- Clerical staff

Budgeted staff in ancillary areas includes some of the following, and may include additional staff at your facility:

- Department manager
- Assistant managers (if applicable)
- Pharmacist
- Physical therapist
- Respiratory therapist
- Technicians

• Assistants
• Clerical staff

The personnel budget is typically a variable budget—the numbers rise and fall depending on the volume and complexity of patient cases. For example, with inpatient areas, salaries increase or decrease depending on the volume of patients on the unit. The opposite of the variable budget is the fixed budget, which remains constant. Some ancillary areas have fixed budgets, but others do not. A fixed budget means that the department has fixed staffing or does not flex staffing with volume fluctuations. Check with your supervisor or finance department to clarify the type of budget you are responsible for and what the expectations are of you managing it.

In both inpatient and outpatient areas, other line items may be fixed, regardless of the volume. For example, if you allot $200 per month for minor equipment, this amount stays the same regardless of the volume of patient cases.

Budgeting methods

Different organizations may have different budgeting practices. For instance, some hospitals use computerized programs to develop their budgets, while others still calculate by hand. With some systems, nurse managers are handed a budget and asked to review, edit, and return it by a certain date; others are expected to perform the "zero-based budget method," or ZBB, requiring the manager to build a budget from scratch.

ZBB

ZBB is the most effective and widely used method for budgeting. It consists of calculating projected costs by line item from the bottom up. In other words, rather than looking at the budget history, the new budget is built upon calculated assumptions. By using this method, you can analyze data and consider alternatives rather than relying solely on the previous year's numbers. (Much of what is covered in the salary portion of expenses throughout this chapter resembles the ZBB method.) But let's look at other models.

Flat percentage increase

The flat percentage increase method begins with a predetermined percentage, which is provided to you. This percentage is then added to the current actual number to determine the budget number. For example, assume that for eight months salaries year-to-date (YTD) are $525,000.

By figuring out the annualized number ($525,000 ÷ 8 months = $65,625 x 12 months = $787,500), you can then move to the next step. Multiply the annualized expense ($787,500) by the predetermined percentage (10%) to calculate next year's increase ($78,750). Add the increase to the annualized expense to reach the total expenses ($866,250) you can plan to pay for the next year.

Although this method is quick and easy, it does not take into consideration productivity, nor does it require analysis. It is important for you to look at the entire picture and learn from the previous year's experiences to produce a credible, realistic budget. Because of this, the ZBB method is most prominent in hospitals.

Computer budgeting software

Another way to calculate budgets is by using sophisticated computer software. Budgeting software has come a long way and is fairly user-friendly. Depending on the software, programs can be fairly expensive, so don't be discouraged if your hospital is not equipped with the software. The most important thing to remember is if your organization is willing to purchase such software, make sure your finance department approves it.

Constructing your budget

Personnel expenses

There are many steps related to determining personnel expenses for your budget. The rest of the chapter discusses 13 steps you can take to calculate these expenses.

Step #1: Gathering data

To prepare your unit's annual budget, at a minimum gather the following data regarding salary expenses:

1. Budgeted UOS or patient days

UOS projections may or may not include your input. Some hospitals give managers the budgeted UOS and then assign them the responsibility of determining the needed personnel and other required resources based on those projections. Other hospitals negotiate with managers to determine UOS. Information used to determine UOS includes the previous year's actual UOS, projections for the upcoming year, and other factors, such as changes in the unit's physical layout, new programs or physicians coming or leaving, and closing or opening of competing hospitals.

If you are told that your UOS are "flat," this means that next year your unit's UOS is expected to remain the same. If you do not agree with the projected or budgeted UOS for your new budget, present data to validate your assumptions (e.g., historical data or information regarding new patient classification types). Present these data early in the budgeting process.

2. Budgeted hours per patient day (HPPD)

To figure salary expenses, you must know the HPPD—or standard of productive, direct-care hours. HPPD is determined in a manner similar to UOS. To figure HPPD, hospitals will also look at benchmarks from national databases (e.g., those of HBSI International, Inc., or nursing associations) and compare the databases' data to the unit's operation figures. When comparing units, make sure what comprises the HPPD in other facilities is the same as in yours. For example, if your unit's HPPD includes orientation and education/training, don't compare your unit to another hospital's that only looks at productive time. Think critically, and be willing to ask questions. Do not just accept these numbers from your finance department. In ancillary areas, the standard may be hours per visit, test, procedure, exam, or other.

For the purposes of calculating HPPD, assume the nursing unit budgeted 67,500 hours the previous year. By dividing the total budgeted hours (67,500) by the UOS (7,500), the HPPD comes to 9.0 (67,500 ÷ 7,500 = 9.0).

3. Average and unit average hourly rates

Some organizations do not give managers the HPPD but the total budgeted hours by job category, whereas others provide only a total salary dollar target and orders for the nurse manager not to be concerned with HPPD. When given the total budgeted hours by job category, determine the average hourly rate for the previous year. To do this, look at the total actual salary dollars for the previous year and divide that amount by the total hours worked. For example, if you paid $1,200,200 in productive salaries and used 65,700 total hours worked by staff, the average hourly rate for the previous year would be $18.27 ($1,200,000 ÷ 65,700 = $18.27).

Rather than breaking down the average hourly rates by job category, set a unit average hourly rate. Add together the hourly rates for each employee, and divide that total by the number of job categories. This number is determined by using the following equation:

(sum of hourly rates) ÷ number of job categories = unit average hourly rate

For example, if the average hourly rate for an RN is $25, for an LPN is $18, and for an NA is $9, then the unit average hourly rate equals $17.33 ([$25 + $18 + $9] ÷ 3 = $17.33). We will use this unit average hourly rate for future examples.

4. Skill mix

Another process you must become involved in is the skill mix breakdown. When determining this breakdown, take into consideration the type of nursing care model (i.e., primary nursing, total patient care, etc.), the hospital policy regarding use of LPNs and NAs, and patient acuity levels. In ancillary areas, the use of technicians or assistants would need to be considered. For the purposes of this book, use the following skill mix percentages: 75% RN, 10% LPN, and 15% NA.

Other considerations when calculating salary expenses

Productive and nonproductive hours

Salary expenses include productive hours (actual time worked or direct-care hours) and non-productive (nonworked) hours. Nonproductive hours include orientation, education, vacation, sick time, holidays, etc. In preparing your budget, allocate required productive, or direct-care, hours. To determine productive hours, use the following equation: UOS x HPPD = total productive hours required

For example, if the annual budgeted UOS is 7,500 and the budgeted HPPD is 9.0, then the total productive hours required is 67,500 (7,500 x 9.0 = 67,500).

Direct and indirect costs

Costs the unit incurs—and that you are responsible for—are called direct costs. Direct costs are those associated with the delivery of patient care. Some direct costs include salaries for RNs, LPNs, NAs, orderlies, and monitor technicians. Other examples of direct costs include supplies, administration fees, and electricity bills.

Indirect costs are those assigned to the unit from other areas. They are costs that are necessary for, but do not directly relate to, the delivery of patient care. For example, services from the biomedical engineering department, or bio-med, fall under indirect costs. For instance, bio-med staff make routine inspections of nursing department equipment. Such maintenance costs are typically charged to the nursing department, because the service was for the unit where the patient received care; therefore, the bio-med department would not be charged.

Budget data

Review the budget data in Figure 3.3. It will be used throughout the chapter.

Sample budget data

Figure 3.3

Medical-surgical/telemetry (Unit has 26 bed capacity)

UOS: 7,500
HPPD: 9.0
Average hourly rate:

	RN:	$25/hour
	LPN:	$18/hour
	NA:	$ 9/hour

Unit average hourly rate: $17.33

Skill mix:

	RN:	75%
	LPN:	10%
	NA:	15%

Step #2: Calculating ADC

Next determine your unit's budgeted average daily census (ADC). ADC is important because it helps you explain variances and project staffing. It is needed also for subsequent calculations throughout this chapter. See the following exercise to get a better understanding of how ADC is calculated.

Exercise

What is your ADC?
UOS ÷ 365 or 7,500 ÷ 365 = 20.55

What is your budgeted occupancy rate?
ADC = 20.55 per day ÷ 26 beds x 100% = 79%

There are 67,500 productive hours budgeted for providing care to the ADC. The ADC represents 20.55 patients per day for 365 days.

Next determine who will provide patient care and how. Remember that not all staff work full time; in fact, if you operate a 12-hour shift unit, each full-time employee will likely work 72 hours per pay period rather than the typical 40 hours.

Step #3: Calculating FTEs

Full-time equivalents (FTE) often suffer from mistaken identity. For instance, FTEs are thought to be people or jobs. In fact, FTEs are positions or hours worked. For example, two part-time RNs working half time will equate to 1 FTE, as their hours worked constitute the same as one full-time employee. One FTE equals 40 hours per week multiplied by 52 weeks, or 2,080 paid hours per year (some hospitals use 2,096 hours to calculate paid hours per year—check with your finance department). Therefore, no matter how many part-time employees work, if their total hours worked equals 80 hours for that two-week pay period, then they equate to one FTE. (See Figure 3.4.)

FTE calculation

Figure 3.4

Hours worked per two-week period ÷ 80 hours = FTE

RN	Hours worked per two-week (80 hours) period		FTE
Sally	80	(80 ÷ 80 = 1.0)	1.0
Joe	72	(72 ÷ 80 = 0.9)	0.9
Steve	64	(64 ÷ 80 = 0.8)	0.8
Nancy	40	(40 ÷ 80 = 0.5)	0.5
Sam	24	(24 ÷ 80 = 0.2)	0.3
Betty	8	(8 ÷ 80 = 0.1)	0.1
How many employees are there?	6		
How many FTEs are there? **3.6 FTEs**			

Now it's time to calculate the number of productive FTEs budgeted for this year. To do this, use the following equation: **total productive hours ÷ number of paid hours within a year for an FTE = total productive FTEs** (67,500 ÷ 2,080 = 32.45 FTEs). This number helps you calculate future data. Based on your HPPD and UOS, your unit is budgeted for 32.45 total productive FTEs.

Calculating FTEs by staffs skill mix

According to Figure 3.3, the unit skill mix is 75% RN, 10% LVN, and 15% NA. Keeping that in mind, break down the FTEs further by their skill or job category. Do this by using the following equations:

• 75% (0.75) x 32.45 = 24.34 RN FTEs

- 10% (0.10) x 32.45 = 3.24 LPN FTEs
- 15% (0.15) x 32.45 = 4.87 NA FTEs

Total = 32.45 FTEs

Step #4: Determining average hourly rate

The average hourly rate becomes more important when determining salaries for the year. By using the average hourly rate, you avoid having to use each staff member's hourly rate. However, for a more accurate calculation of salary expenses for next year, use each staff member's salary. Because this process is time-consuming, we will use the average hourly rate for the RN, LPN, and NA job categories in this book.

The average hourly rate can be obtained from numerous sources. Look at your recent labor distribution report, staffing offices computer-generated reports, or payroll department report. No matter how you obtain the average hourly rate, make sure you do, because it's necessary for determining total direct salaries. Be sure to get the average hourly rate for each job category.

Figure 3.3 shows our assumptions for the sample medical-surgical/telemetry unit. Remember to factor in any projected merit increases/raises. To figure out the rate for each category, first determine the hours you will project for each productive category by using the following equations:

- RN total hours: 75% of 67,500 = 50,625 hours (0.75 x 67,500 = 50,625)
- LPN total hours: 10% of 67,500 = 6,750 hours (0.10 x 67,500 = 6,750)
- NA total hours: 15% of 67,500 = 10,125 hours (0.15 x 67,500 = 10,125)

Step #5: Calculating salary dollars by skill mix

In Figure 3.5 you will find the hours worked by each skill category (i.e., RN, LPN, and NA), the categories average hourly pay rate, and the total direct salaries you must account for in the department's budget.

Figure 3.5	Sample total salaries calculation

Hours x average hourly rate = Total direct salaries

RN: 50,625 x $25 =	$1,265,625
LPN: 6,750 x $18 =	$121,500
NA: 10,125 x $9 =	$91,125
Total direct salary dollars =	**$1,478,250**

When using the unit average hourly rate, use following calculation:

67,500 x $17.33 =	$1,169,775

As you can see, by using the "average hourly rate" in the equation, you are able to get a more accurate projection for salaries than when using the unit average hourly rate.

Step #6: Determining replacement needs

Figuring replacement hours by skill category

Using the information found in Figure 3.5, the nursing unit plans to spend approximately $1,478,250 for direct-care staff salaries for the year. However, when preparing your budget, remember that staff will take time off, and their replacement must be accounted for. To do this, first figure out the nonproductive hours, which will later be used to determine the cost of the replacement. The industry average for the percentage of nonproductive hours making up the total paid hours is 15%–20%. That means that 15%–20% of the money paid toward staff salaries is for nonproductive time (i.e., orientation, education, vacation, sick time, and holidays). This percentage varies depending on several factors such as the number of paid holidays the organization offers its employees as a benefit and orientation/education practices. The percentage of nonproductive hours is necessary when figuring FTEs and calculating the cost of salaries for the budget.

When budgeting for replacements, use 18% as the average (18% is the midpoint between 15%–20%, the industry average). This means that 18% of the time, the employee from this skill or job category will not be working. Therefore, replace 18% of that time and cost for each staff category. See Figure 3.6.

Calculating replacement FTEs

```
┌─ Figure 3.6 ─────────────────────────────────────────────────────────────────────────────────┐
│                                                                                                 │
│  For varied skill mix                                                                           │
│  How many replacement FTEs do you need?                                                         │
│  18% (0.18) x RN FTEs (24.34) = 4.4 FTEs                                                         │
│  18% x LPN FTEs (3.24) = 0.58 FTEs                                                               │
│  18% x NA FTEs (4.87) = 0.88 FTEs                                                               │
│  Total additional FTEs needed for replacement: 5.86                                             │
│                                                                                                 │
│  For balanced skill mix                                                                         │
│  If staff skill mix is balanced at 50%/50% (i.e., 50% are RNs and 50% are LPNs), another way to calculate for replacement FTEs is by │
│  using the following equation:                                                                  │
│  Total FTEs x average replacement needed = Total additional FTEs needed for replacement         │
│  (32.45 x 0.18 = 5.84)                                                                          │
│                                                                                                 │
└─────────────────────────────────────────────────────────────────────────────────────────────┘
```

Now that you have figured out the additional FTEs needed for replacement staff, determine the new totals for the FTEs needed for next year.

RN: 24.34 + 4.4 = 28.74

LPN: 3.24 + 0.58 = 3.82

NA: 4.87 + 0.88 = 5.75

Total projected FTEs: 38.31

Now it's time to determine the amount of additional salaries that must be accounted for (nonproductive replacement) in the budget. See Figure 3.7.

Determining nonproductive replacement

```
┌─ Figure 3.7 ─────────────────────────────────────────────────────────────────────────────────┐
│                                                                                                 │
│  How much additional salary do you need to pay for staff's allotted time off?                   │
│  Total direct salaries x average replacement needed = Nonproductive replacement ($1,478,250 (see Figure 3.5) x 0.18 = │
│  $266,085)                                                                                      │
│  Total additional salaries needed for replacement (nonproductive replacement) of 5.86 FTEs: $266,085 │
│                                                                                                 │
└─────────────────────────────────────────────────────────────────────────────────────────────┘
```

Let's calculate the amount of productive hours per FTE. See Figure 3.8.

Calculating productive hours per FTE

```
┌─ Figure 3.8 ─────────────────────────────────────────────────────────────────────────────────┐
│                                                                                                 │
│              Adding cost of nonproductive replacement and additional FTEs to productive         │
│                                                                                                 │
│  Total direct salary dollars: $1,478,250            Total FTEs: 32.45 FTEs                       │
│  Total nonproductive replacement: $266,085          Total nonprod. replacement: 5.86 FTEs       │
│  New total salaries: $1,744,335                     Total FTEs: 38.31 FTEs                       │
│                                                                                                 │
└─────────────────────────────────────────────────────────────────────────────────────────────┘
```

Because we are using 18% as an average for replacement, we know that 82% (100% –18% = 82%) of the total paid 2,080 hours per FTE are productive. This is figured by multiplying the total paid hours per FTE by the percent of productive hours (2,080 x 82%). Therefore, there are **1,706 productive hours per FTE**. The remainder of the 2,080 hours per employee is used for vacations, holidays, sick time, etc.

Step #7: Determining expenses for indirect positions

For this example, assume the nurse manager and the monitor technician positions remain Because the monitor technician is a 1.0 FTE on days, evenings, and nights and requires replacement, determine the total FTEs for this position by using the 18% replacement factor calculated earlier. For example, multiply the average replacement needed (18%) by monitor technician FTEs (3.0) to reach the nonproductive replacement (3.0 x 0.18 = 0.54). Then calculate the number of monitor technician FTEs by doing the following equation: 3.0 + 0.54 = 3.54 monitor technician FTEs. See Figure 3.9.

Sample position control

Figure 3.9

Position control for medical-surgical/telemetry unit

	Approved	Filled	Status
Fixed staff			
Nurse manager	1.0		
Monitor technician	3.54		
Total fixed staff	**4.54**		
Variable staff			
RN (includes charge nurse)	28.73 (75% of 38.31)		
LPN	3.83 (10% of 38.31)		
NA	5.75 (15% of 38.31)		
Total variable staff	**38.31**		
Total positions	**42.85 FTEs**		

To update the position control, list currently filled positions and their status. This allows you to see which positions are open. See Figure 3.10.

Updated position control for med-surg/telemetry unit

Figure 3.10

Position control for medical-surgical/telemetry unit

	Approved	Filled	Status
Fixed staff			
Nurse manager	1.0	1.0	0
Monitor technician	3.54	3.25	-0.29
Total fixed staff	4.54	4.25	-0.29
Variable staff			
RN (includes charge nurse)	28.73	26.75	-1.98
LPN	3.83	3.83	0
NA	5.75	6.0	+0.25
Total variable staff	38.31	36.58	-1.73
Total positions:	**42.85**	**Total filled: 40.83**	**Total open: 2.02**

\+ FTEs are over the approved number

\- FTEs are under the approved number

You have calculated the direct salaries and replacements for the above salaries and FTEs. As you can see, other positions are considered indirect, as they do not provide hands-on patient care and are not part of the daily staffing hours. In this example, the nurse manager and monitor technician are considered indirect.

When adding the nurse manager and monitor technician's salaries, assume the nurse manager earns $75,000 per year and the technician makes $10 per hour. To figure out how much of the budget can be spent on the monitor technician's position, multiply the approved FTE (3.54) by the pay rate of the position. Then multiply that total by the number of hours per year (2,080; 3.54 x $10 x 2,080 = $73,632). Because the nurse manager is an FTE of 1.0 and is a salaried (or exempt) staff member, you do not have to multiply the salary amount by 2,080. To determine the total amount of indirect salary expenses that must be added to the current salary subtotal, add the two numbers together ($75,000 + $73,632 = **$148,632**). See Figure 3.11.

Determining total salaries

Figure 3.11

Total direct salaries:	$1,478,250	(See Figure 3.5)
Total nonproductive replacement:	$266,085	(See Figure 3.7)
Subtotal salaries:	$1,744,335	
Indirect staff salaries:	$148,632	(See calculation above)
Total salaries:	$1,892,967	

Step #8: Calculating skill mix of staff per shift

Now that you have figured out staff salaries, determine the skill mix of staff per shift. Remember that in some states, such as California, staffing ratios are mandated by law and dictate that nurses can only care for a specified number of patients at one time. It is likely that, in the future, other states will follow California's lead, so keep your ears and eyes open for changing legislation. For the purposes of the following exercise, assume that no such ratios exist. To determine skill mix, take factors such as your hospital's policy, the level of patient acuity, patient care history, and staff competency, into consideration.

Your next action is to determine what percentage of nursing staff work days (7 a.m.–3 p.m.), evenings (3 p.m.–11 p.m.), and nights (11 p.m.–7 a.m.). Collaborate with staff when deciding the percentage of staff to work on each shift. For example, if the day shift is the busiest, consider putting most of your staff on the day shift. In units where activity does not change from shift to shift and shifts are generally eight hours long, (i.e., critical care), the allocation may be 33%/33%/33%. This is because work is evenly distributed among all shifts. Keep in mind that most activities occur during day and evening shifts.

For an active, 12-hour shift unit (i.e., in an intensive care unit), it may be 50%/50%. As nurse manager, you control this number and can make changes based on the unit's activity. However, you should involve your staff when deciding the best way to distribute work over the 24-hour period. Because each organization is different, there are no set standards for staff distribution except in areas mandated by regulations. For this example, use the information given in Figure 3.12. Also for this example, assume the following information is true:

- Budgeted ADC: 20.55
- HPPD: 9.0
- 75% of the staff are RNs
- 10% of the staff are LPNs
- 15% of the staff are NAs

Percentage of staff for each shift

Figure 3.12

Percentage of staff working days, evenings, and nights for medical-surgical/telemetry unit

1. Total direct-care hours ÷ number of days in a year = total hours of care per day
   67,500 ÷ 365 = 184.93 hours of care per day
2. Total hours of care per day ÷ length of shift = shifts for 24-hour period
   184.93 ÷ 8 hours shifts = 23.12 shifts
3. Ask staff to make a list of tasks and activities that occur routinely on each shift. This list should include medications, procedures, physician visits, orders, baths, ambulation, etc. The number of tasks per shift will determine the percentage of staff needed on each shift. For example, there are a total of 100 tasks: 40 performed on the day shift, 35 on the evening shift, and 25 on the night shift.

Staff distribution by shift: 40% days, 35% evenings, 25% nights

The amount of hours of care per day (184.93) helps you calculate the number of staff members needed to care for the ADC of 20.55 patients for seven days a week, 365 days a year. Remember FTEs are not shifts or people; they are positions or hours worked. To see what a 24-hour period would look like using the information calculated in Figure 3.12, review the chart in Figure 3.13. Using the following assumptions, you will be able to calculate how many shifts your department is allowed for a 24-hour period:

- Budgeted ADC: 20.55
- Total direct-care hours: 67,500
- Skill mix: 75% RN, 10% LPN, 15% NA
- Shift lengths: Eight hours
- Staff distribution by shift: 40% of X work days, 35% of X work evenings, 25% of X work nights

Use the following data to fill in the chart:

1. Total shifts for a 24-hour period

67,500 ÷ 365 days = 184.93 hours per day ÷ eight-hour shifts = 23.12 shifts for a 24-hour period

2. Shifts per staff category for a 24-hour period
- RN: 75% of 23.12 = 17.34 RN shifts for 24 hours
- LPN: 10% of 23.12 = 2.31 LPN shifts for 24 hours
- NA: 15% of 23.12 = 3.47 NA shifts for 24 hours

3. Number of staff needed to work shift (Finkler and Kovner 2000)

Days:

- 40% of the 17.34 RN shifts = 6.94
- 40% of the 2.31 LPN shifts = 0.92
- 40% of the 3.47 NA shifts = 1.39

Evenings:

- 35% of the 17.34 RN shifts = 6.07
- 35% of the 2.31 LPN shifts = 0.81
- 35% of the 3.47 NA shifts = 1.21

Nights:

- 25% of the 17.34 RN shifts = 4.34
- 25% of the 2.31 LPN shifts = 0.58
- 25% of the 3.47 NA shifts = 0.87

Figure 3.13   **Calculating the number of shifts needed per 24 hours**

Shift			Day (40%)	Evening (35%)	Night (25%)	Total
RN	(75%)	17.34	6.94	6.07	4.34	
LPN	(10%)	2.31	0.92	0.81	0.58	
NA	(15%)	3.47	1.39	1.21	0.87	
Total			**9.25**	**8.09**	**5.79**	**23.13**

After plotting the calculated numbers, you will notice figures such as 0.92 and 1.39. These figures represent the number of shifts that must be filled and the amount of RNs, LPNs, or NAs needed to do so. Decide whether to round such figures up or down. For instance, for the day shift, you are allowed to fill the schedule with 6.94 RNs, 0.92 LPNs, or 1.39 NAs. You decide whether to schedule six RNs, one LPN, and two NAs or seven RNs, one LPN, and one NA. Whatever you decide, be sure to base your decision on important factors such as your state's staffing regulations, department activity, and nurse competency.

Figure 3.14 is a revised chart with rounded numbers.

Figure 3.14

Number of shifts allowed per 24 hours

Shift		Day (40%)	Evening (35%)	Night (25%)	Total
RN	(75%) 17.34	7	6	4	
LPN	(10%) 2.31	1	1	1	
NA	(15%) 3.47	1	1	1	
Total		9	8	6	23

Total number of shifts allowed per 24 hours: 23.13 shifts

Additional expenses

Additional salary expenses to add to the budget include shift differentials such as weekend bonuses, orientation, and benefits.

Step #9: Calculating differentials

Differentials are costs the hospital pays to entice staff to work on the nonprime-time shifts such as evenings, nights, weekends, and holidays. Some hospitals will even pay a differential to nurses willing to fill in as charge nurse. Differentials are used for those and other creative incentives to persuade staff to cover shifts they would not normally work. Every hospital pays some form of differential, so it's important that you add these costs into your budget. Earlier, we calculated the average hourly rate, which was calculated on base hourly pay only. When calculating the average hourly rate for your unit, remember to include differentials in your math. For the sake of this example, assume the hospital pays the following differential for its medical-surgical/telemetry unit:

Staff	Shift	Other
RN	3 p.m.–11 p.m.	$2.00
RN	11 p.m.–7 a.m.	$3.00
LPN	3 p.m.–11 p.m.	$1.50
LPN	11 p.m.–7 a.m.	$2.00
NA	3 p.m.–11 p.m.	$1.00
NA	11 p.m.–7 a.m.	$1.50

Remember that 40% of staff work the day shift, 35% work the evening shift, and 25% work the night shift. Use this information to calculate the additional salaries needed and add the sum to the salary subtotal. In other words, 40% of the staff will receive no differential because they are on the prime-time shift, 35% of the staff will receive the evening-shift differential, and 25% of the staff will receive the night-shift differential.

Determine the cost of such differentials by using the information we already have regarding skill mix and percentage of staff per shift. See Figures 3.15, 3.16, 3.17, and 3.18.

Figure 3.15

Calculating RN differential salary costs for evenings and nights

Total RN FTEs x percent that working shift = RN FTEs for the shift

Direct FTEs for RN: 75%
Total RN FTEs: 28.73
Work on evening shift: 35%   28.73 x 0.35 = 10.06 RN FTEs for the evening shift
Work on night shift: 25%   28.73 x 0.25 = 7.18 RN FTEs for the night shift
Average hourly rate (See Figure 3.3 on page 48): $25/hour
RN FTE for the shift x differential expense x number of hours per year = differential salary expenses for RNs
Evening shift: 10.06 x $2 x 2,080 = **$41,850**
Night shift: 7.18 x $3 x 2,080 = **$44,803**

Figure 3.16

Calculating LPN differential salary costs for evenings and nights

Total LPN x percent that working shift = LPN FTEs for the shift

Direct FTEs for LPN: 10%
Total LPN FTEs: 3.82
Work on evening shift: 35%   3.82 x 0.35 = 1.34 LPN FTEs for the evening shift
Work on night shift: 25%   3.82 x 0.25 = 0.96 LPN FTEs for the night shift
Average hourly rate: $18/hour
LPN for the shift x differential expense x number of hours per year = differential salary expenses for LPNs
Evening shift: 1.34 x $1.50 x 2,080 = **$4,181**
Night shift: 0.96 x $2 x 2,080 = **$3,994**

Calculating NA FTEs differential salary costs for evenings and nights

Figure 3.17

Total NA FTEs x percent that working shift = NA FTEs for the shift

Direct FTEs for NA: 15%
Total NA FTEs: 5.75
Work on evening shift: 35%   5.75 x 0.35 = 2.01 NA FTEs for the evening shift
Work on night shift: 25%   5.75 x 0.25 = 1.43 NA FTEs for the night shift
Average hourly rate: $9/hour
NA FTE for the shift x differential expense x number of hours per year = Differential salary expenses for NAs
Evening shift: 2.01 x $1 x 2,080 = **$4,180**
Night shift: 1.43 x $1.50 x 2,080 = **$4,462**

Total shift differentials

Figure 3.18

	Evening shift		Night shift
RN	$41,850		$44,803
LPN	4,181		3,994
NA	4,180		4,462
Total	50,211	+	53,259 = **$103,470**

Step #10: Totaling salaries

Now that you've calculated shift differentials, retally the total for salaries and the budget. (See Step #6)

Total direct salaries:	$1,478,250
Total nonproductive replacement:	266,085
Subtotal salaries:	$1,744,335
Indirect staff salaries from above:	148,632
Total salaries:	$1,892,967
Shift differentials:	103,470
New total:	**$1,996,437**

If your hospital pays additional differentials to nurses filling in as charge nurses—above and beyond their normal salary—remember to add in the additional expenses to the final total. If the differential is $2.00 per hour and you use an average of 10 nurses per month on 8 hour shifts, the formula would be the following:

10 nurses x 8 hours x $2 = $8,320

Step #11: Figuring benefits

Benefits, or fringe benefits, are the last wages calculated and added to this section of expenses. Benefits are special perks given to those employed by the hospital. Such benefits may include medical, dental, vision, and life insurance. They also include pension and Social Security.

Today, benefits constitute 25%–35% of salary expenses. Check with the finance department for your hospitals benefits percentage. For this example, use the benefits percentage of 30%. Add benefits to the total direct and indirect salary expense. To figure the amount of the budget spent on benefits, multiply the total salary expense by the percentage of benefits ($1,996,437 x 30% = $598,931).

Step #12: Calculating overtime

Pay close attention to incremental overtime. For instance, if staff routinely stay late to complete patient charts, talk, etc., their extra overtime minutes can add up.

If your hospital allows you to budget for overtime—some hospitals do not—review the previous year's data for your unit and calculate overtime at the hospital's overtime rate of pay. For example, if the overtime rate is time and a half and an RN makes $25/hour, the overtime rate of pay is $37.50/hour. To figure out how much overtime the RN would make, multiply the overtime rate of pay by the number of hours of overtime projected and the total added to the salaries. For example, assume each RN works an average of 10 overtime hours per year. Use the following formula to calculate the cost of overtime:

Average overtime hours per year (10 hours) X overtime rate ($37.50) X the RN FTE (28.73) = Total cost of RN overtime (10 x $37.50 x 28.73 = $10,774).

Scheduled overtime is the overtime that is planned for in your budget. It can be the last four hours of a 12-hour shift or planned extra shifts. Some facilities are strict about overtime and only allow scheduled or 12-hour shift overtime be budgeted with the understanding that the manager will control it on the unit. In such cases, overtime is not allowed unless it is an emergency. However, this practice is hospital-specific, so ask about your organization's policy. For this book, assume that no overtime has been budgeted for the coming year.

Step #13: Determining orientation and education/training costs

Orientation is the period of time set aside for new hires to learn unit policies and procedures and to become acclimated with its activities. Orientation consists of reading policies, observing experienced nurses, performing return demonstrations of tasks, caring for patients under supervision, and gaining understanding of unit practice standards.

When budgeting for orientation, either set money aside to pay for it or combine it with education. In some cases, orientation even may fall under productive hours. (It is important to understand where these orientation dollars are located so you can budget accordingly.) For instance, if you expect to absorb the orientation costs into productive HPPD, then factor this into your schedule. In other words, leave a buffer for those days when you have orientees on the unit. (To view six questions to keep in mind regarding orientation, go to the Chapter 3 folder on your CD-ROM.)

Critical thinking

For this activity, assume that education, training, and orientation are separate from the HPPD and have a line item to themselves.

Facts:

- You will hire five new RNs and one LPN this year
- Each new RN and LPN requires six weeks of orientation on the day shift
- You will hire two new NAs this year
- Each new NA requires four weeks of orientation on the day shift
- Everyone on the staff is entitled to five paid education days per year
- All staff are paid to attend six two-hour-long staff meetings
- All staff are paid to attend four hours of cardiopulmonary resuscitation (CPR) training
- All RNs must take an eight-hour advanced cardiac life support (ACLS) course every two years

See Figures 3.19, 3.20, and 3.21.

Calculating orientation costs for new hires

Figure 3.19

Number of hires X length of orientation (in hours) X average hourly rate = total orientation costs
RN: 5 x 6 weeks (240 hours) x $25 = $ 30,000
LPN: 1 x 6 weeks (240 hours) x $18 = $4,320
NA: 2 x 4 weeks (160 hours) x $9 = $2,880
Total hours: 640 (total hours) ÷ by 2,080 = additional 0.3 FTE of staff for orientation. This number (0.3) must be added to the total budgeted FTEs.

Calculating education and training costs for staff

Figure 3.20

FTE X paid education hours + (CPR training hours + staff meeting hours) = Total education and training hours A
5 days = 40 hours, 4 hours + 12 hours = 16 hours, 40 + 12 = 56 hours
RN: 28.74 x 56 hours = 1,609 hours
Because the eight-hour ACLS is required every two years, you will budget 50% for the first year and 50% for the second. Therefore, only 50% of RNs will take the course this year.
50% of RNs x hours of ACLS training = Total education and training hours B
50% of RNs (14.37) x 8 = 114.96, or 115 hours
(Total education and training hours A + total education and training hours B) x average hourly rate = total education and training costs
(1,609 + 115) x $25 = $43,100
FTE X paid education hours + (CPR training hours + staff meeting hours) x average hourly rate = total education and training hours
LPN: 3.82 x 56 hours x $18 = $3,851
NA: 5.75 x 56 hours x $9 = $2,898

Calculating total orientation and education/training costs

Figure 3.21

Total orientation costs + total education/training costs = total orientation and education/training costs
RN: $30,000 + 43,100 = $73,100
LPN: $4,320 + $3,851 = $8,171
NA: $2,880 + $2,898 = $5,778
Total orientation and education/training costs for RN + total for LPN + total for NA = total orientation and education/training costs
$73,100 + $8,171 + $5,778 = $87,049
You must add $87,049 orientation and education/training costs to the 2005 budget.

Now, total up the salaries for the budget:

Total direct salaries:	$1,478,250
Total nonproductive replacement:	266,085
Subtotal salaries:	$1,744,335
Indirect staff salaries from above:	148,632

Subtotal salaries:	$1,892,967
Shift differentials:	103,470
Benefits:	598,931
Subtotal salaries:	$2,595,368
Orientation:	87,049
Grand total salaries:	$2,682,417

Variable costs vs. fixed costs

For budgeting purposes, all costs are considered to be either fixed or variable. A variable cost is a cost or expense that is incurred as a direct result of volume (i.e., increased census). A fixed cost is one the unit will experience regardless of the volume or activity (i.e., the electricity bill). The following are examples of both:

Variable costs	Fixed costs
Personnel	Electricity
Education	Depreciation
Food	Preventative maintenance
Supplies	Xerox rental
Linen	Nurse manager salary

Variable costs are budgeted based on the UOS. That is because supply use increases and decreases with patient census. Fixed costs, on the other hand, are often divided and budgeted as a flat monthly rate.

When budgeting for nonsalary items such as supplies, the finance department should provide you with an "inflation factor." (If they do not, however, you must do the necessary research to obtain the number.) The inflation factor is a predetermined number accounting for price increases for the coming year. For the purposes of this chapter, assume the inflation factor is 6%.

Annualizing costs

One of the most common methods for annualizing costs is to look at the year-to-date (YTD) data on the most current departmental reports. "Annualizing" allows you to estimate the end-of-the-year, or YTD, numbers based on the unit's monthly history. Assuming there is data for the past eight months, to project expenses for the upcoming year, divide the YTD total—which is found on the departmental financial statement/cost-center report—by eight to get an average monthly expense. Then, multiply the sum by 12 months to reach an annualized number. For example, the YTD expenses for supplies is $35,000.

YTD expense ÷ number of months of data = average monthly expense X number of months in a year = annualized expense ($35,000 ÷ 8 = $4,375 x 12 = $52,500)

Although this method is not always exact, it does give you an estimate for average monthly expenses. After calculating the average for eight months of data, try to think of any significant expenses that may be incurred for the next four months that would be reflected in the average. If any, add them into the total. For example, if the average monthly expense is $4,375 and next month you expect to add a large volume of a new supply item to the supply cart, add this amount to the supply budget total. (See Figure 3.22.)

Methods for annualizing costs and planning expenses

> **Figure 3.22**
>
> **Methods for annualizing costs and planning next year's expenses**
> **Total fixed cost expenses YTD x 8 months x 12 months = Annualized figure**
>
> Fixed costs:
> Bio-med costs for the last 8 months = $2,500.
> ($2,500 ÷ 8) x 12 months = $3,750 annualized figure
> For next year's budget:
> **Annualized figure x inflation factor = Expenses for next year's budget**
> $3,750 x 6% (1.06) = $3,975 for next year's budget

Supplies

To determine supply expenses for the unit, review Figure 3.23.

Supply budgeting for a nursing unit

> **Figure 3.23**
>
> For the first eight months of this year, your unit consumed the following in supplies:
> Medical = $23,967
> $23,967 ÷ 8 x 12 = $35,951 x 1.06 = **$38,108 projected for next year**
> Nonmedical = $12,006
> $12,006 ÷ 8 x 12 = $18,009 x 1.06 = **$19,090 projected for next year**

Test your critical thinking skills by figuring out what the projected expenses are for 2008. This exercise is in the Chapter 3 folder on your CD-ROM.

Plugging in your budget numbers

Now it's time to plot the above figures into your budget. See the example for the medical-surgical/telemetry unit in Figure 3.24.

2009 budget for medical-surgical/telemetry unit

Figure 3.24	

Medical-surgical/telemetry unit budget for 2009

Patient days	**7,500**
Revenue	**5,950,000**
Expenses	
Direct salaries	$1,478,250
Nonproductive salaries	266,085
Indirect salaries	148,632
Differentials/bonuses	103,470
Orientation/training	87,049
Overtime	0
Employee benefits	598,931
Total salaries	**$2,682,417**
Medical supplies	38,108
Nonmedical supplies	19,090
Minor equipment	1,800
Equipment rental	807
Maintenance	1,506
Bio-med	3,975
Linen	14,080
Nutritional support	20,948
Interdepartmental transfers	23,889
Other	1,109
Total other expenses	**125,312**
Total expenses	**$2,807,729**

Capital budgets

A capital budget is one that outlines projected buying of large, fixed assets or equipment that depreciates such as MRI or ultrasound machines. What qualifies as a capital expense varies among organizations; however, generally, it is any piece of equipment that is worth more than $500 and has a lifespan of five years.

The capital budget is separate from the operating budget and requires all requests for capital equipment be approved by a budget committee. Granted requests must meet the goals and objectives of the hospital.

If you are responsible for developing a capital budget, you may have to fill out a form called the "capital budget acquisition form." Such forms are used when requesting funding for new equipment. They are used to make the case for purchasing new, large price-tag items and equipment.

BONUS TOOLS

To view a sample capital budget acquisition form, look in the Chapter 3 folder on your CD-ROM.

Position control

The position control, or position budget (approved positions), discussed in step #7, is an important document and resource, second only to the budget itself. The position control identifies each job category, the number of budgeted FTEs, and whether projections are on target or there are vacant positions. The position control also indicates whether there are too many positions for a particular job category.

The position control comes in several varieties, and it was long thought that its only purpose was to serve as the "hiring plan" for the unit and for human resources (HR). However, when it is used as the translation of the budget into the defined "scheduling requirements" for the unit, it takes on greater importance in providing staffing for safe patient outcomes because there is consistent evidence for an association between the level of nursing staffing and patient outcomes.

Be sure to update the position control regularly as it changes each budget year or as your number of FTEs and skill mix change. In fact, update the position control each time a person is hired or when an employee resigns, transfers, or changes status.

Minimum, good, and best position control management

According to the Labor Management Institute, at a minimum, position control management addresses filled and open positions compared to hired and actual FTE positions.

Good position control addresses the minimum requirements as well as:

- Incorporates or references the budgeted FTEs by skill mix

- Positions by job codes or classes or skill mix (e.g., RN, LPN, NA) for direct care (defined as those that are part of the variable staffing plan providing hands-on care to the patient)

- Positions by job codes or classes or skill mix for indirect care (defined as those that are paid from the cost center but are not part of the variable staffing plan, [also called fixed staff])

The "best" position control will include:

1. Job codes to track budgeted dollars for your FTE positions

2. Hire dates for the employees in the filled positions to track issues regarding seniority

3. Designation for full-time (FT) or part-time (PT) status as a check for your optimum or budgeted FT/PT rotation plan

4. Position control numbering schemas that allow for "loaning" filled positions to other units for some period (e.g., a diabetic educator that is hired to a unit for a diabetic education program that gets put on hold)

5. Position control reports that provide:

- Tracking by shift as a check against your budgeted "care distribution hours"

- Position tracking for weekday and weekend distribution to:

  - Compare your budgeted positions to the schedule at posting to visually check that youhave distributed your resources to the shifts to which they are budgeted

  - Compare your budgeted positions to the schedule after the schedule is posted to visually establish where your resources ended up working, especially if you use self-scheduling in your unit (or selfish scheduling, depending on your unit-based guidelines and employee requests)

- Comparison of actual to budget paid FTEs with variance

- Comparison of actual worked FTEs to the target or variable staffing plan FTEs with variance

- Comparison of actual and budget workload for productivity reference (e.g., how busy the unit was for the period being evaluated)

Please refer to the position control example shown in Figure 3.25, which is the summary portion of the position control plan that demonstrates, integrates, and compares the unit's budget to the position control plan. It also contains the budgeted-job codes, the position control numbers (e.g., 902.691.1201.1966.1) that incorporate the unit's cost center (902), the job code (e.g., 691), and the employee's hire date.

Position Control Example

Figure 3.25

	Total	700	1500	2300	Non-productive data		Per day	700	1500	2300
Unit Budget FTEs	43.7	14.6	14.6	14.6	Budget NP%	9.70%				
Position control FTEs	43.7	14.6	14.6	14.6	Budget NP hours	8,819.20	24	8	8	8
Hired FTEs	40.8				Budget NP FTEs	4.24				
Direct HPPD	19.5	6.5	6.5	6.5	Unit replacement NP FTE allocation	2.24	12.73			
Total HPPD	22.7	7.6	7.6	7.6	Resource Pool NP FTE Allocation	2	12			

Job Title	Job Code	Position Number	PC FTE	Hired FTE	Var. FTE	Filed By	Hire Date	Status	0700 Pos. Hours	1500 Pos. Hours	2300 Pos. Hours
RN Weekend Program											
	691	902.691.12011996.1	0.9	0.9	0	PT	12-01-1996	FT		32	40
	692	902.692.12121999.1	0.9	0.9	0	JC	12-12-1999	FT	9.35	12.15	10.3
		Filled RN Positions	31.8	31.8	0.05						
		902.682.00000000.1	1	0	-1	Vacant					80
		902.682.00000000.2	1	0	-1	Vacant					80
		902.682.00000000.3	0.2	0	-0.2	Vacant					16
		Vacant RN Positions	2.2	0	2.3				0	0	2.2
		Total RN's=34.1	34.1	31.8	2.3				9.35	12.15	12.6
		Total RNs	34.1	31.8	2.3						
		Total Care Partners	3	2.5	0.6						
		Total Direct	37.1	34.2	2.9						
		Total Indirect	6.6	6.6	0						
		Total FTEs	43.7	40.8	2.9				14.55	14.55	14.6

Overtime in excess of 5% is associated with adverse patient outcomes (medication errors and patient falls) based on research conducted by the Labor Management Institute, so position control reports that can tell us how efficiently and effectively we are scheduling and staffing our resources should help us to promote safe staffing for our patients. I recommend the Position Control Best Practice Guidelines developed by the Labor Management Institute. See Figure 3.26 for the Labor Management Institute's criteria to help you evaluate your position control.

Labor Management Institute best practices position control

Figure 3.26

Name: _____   Unit name: _____

Instructions: As a manager, please indicate if you are provided the criteria necessary to evaluate your position control comments. Thank you.

Criteria for evaluation of cost center position control:	Responses Yes	No
1. Based on the budgeted FTE's		
2. Includes filled and unfilled (vacant FTE's)		
3. Includes category of staff (job codes/classes) or skill mix (for example, caregiver groups such as direct: RN, LPN, NA, other and indirect: e.g., unit manager, secretary)		
4. Includes date of hire for seniority tracking		
5. Includes positions for both full-time and part-time work agreements		
6. Allows positions to be distributed by shifts (days, pm, and nights)		
7. Allows positions to be distributed on weekends		
8. Compares budgeted positions to filled positions		
9. Compares actual hours worked by shift to the budgeted position		
10. Compares overtime by shift to the budgeted position		
11. Compares agency/traveler hours by shift to the budgeted positions		
12. Compares actual and budgeted census or other workload for the reporting period		
13. Is manged by the unit manager		
14. Is shared by HR as the unit's hiring plan		
15. Is shared by finance for FTE management		
16. Is integrated to and updated automatically by HR, payroll, and workload information		
17. Provides reports that have been updated from integrated system data		

Source: 2002-2007 © Labor Management Institute and ChrysMarie Suby. Used with permission.

Once you determine the number of FTEs needed for the budget, develop a list of positions broken down by category. See Figure 3.9 for a sample position control for the medical-surgical/telemetry unit. Remember, the med-surg/telemetry unit has an ADC of 20.55 and 32.45 FTEs for direct caregivers. The position control includes fixed staff members who do not necessarily provide hands-on care but are in place regardless of the census. Such staffs will not vary as the census fluctuates.

Chapter 4

BUDGET PRESENTATION

Learning objectives

After reading this chapter, the learner will be able to:

- Describe breakdown analysis
- Define controllable costs
- Explain how to manage controllable costs

Presentation skills

Now that you have reviewed the concepts behind budgets and know how to build your own, it's time to learn the skills you need to successfully present your budget.

> **TIP**
>
> Practice your budget presentation with a peer, your director, or the chief nurse executive (CNE) before presenting it to the committee. This person can ask questions, which allows you to prepare answers before heading into the formal presentation. Doing a practice presentation also allows you to strengthen your presentation and public-speaking skills.

Presenting your budget to a supervisor or committee

First you must present the budget to your supervisor or the committee so the appropriate people can sign off on what you have proposed. Remember: No matter who signs off on the budget, you are held accountable for any discrepancies.

> **TIP**
>
> A budget is a budget. Never say "the budget is wrong." If there are discrepancies, indicate that you will provide a description of the issue or variance. Then develop an action plan to address the issue.

During the budget presentation, you will be asked whether the unit met its goals and objectives from the previous year. Be prepared to answer this question by explaining the current status of the goals and objectives as well as sharing your plans to modify the goals or develop new ones for the coming year.

Next review the year-to-date (YTD) numbers from the current budget. The committee wants to know whether the YTD, or actual, numbers are above or below what you budgeted. Your job then is to explain any variances.

Monthly monitoring of the budget is crucial for being ready to answer the committee's questions. By spotting trends and variances early, you can take advantage of opportunities or stop problems in their path. Either way, staying on top of your budget is the best preparation you can do.

> **TIP**
>
> Bring data with you to your meeting. Trends that are depicted in a graph or a chart can be compelling. For example, if you can show that between 10 a.m. and 2 p.m. each day for six months your unit received 10 admissions, discharges, and transfers this will provide you with data to build your case for more staff.

After presenting your YTD numbers, discuss new programs or goals you either have established or wish to establish for next year. The bottom line: You need to be prepared for these discussions.

BONUS TOOLS

For sample scenarios that will help when defending your budget, as well as tips on what never to say to the CFO, refer back to the bonus tools in the Chapter 3 folder on this book's accompanying CD-ROM.

Variance analysis

As mentioned earlier, variances are the difference between budgeted amounts and actual amounts. You must explain any variances on your monthly financial statements. Some organizations require managers to explain all variances, while others only require explanations for variances found in salaries, overtime, supplies, purchased services, or professional fees (i.e., any outside agency expense such as travel nurses or other agency staff, dues, subscriptions, outside education).

Do not waste time analyzing the areas you have little control over, such as revenue or benefits. Instead, focus your energy on what you do control—staffing patterns, overtime, and the skill mix. In some hospitals, nurse managers must explain variances above 105% or below 95%, so know exactly what is expected of you before you begin your variance analysis. When doing your expense analysis, remember that variances over 100% are bad—this means you spent more than was budgeted. However, variances under 100% mean you spent less than was budgeted.

Remember to expect that when units of service (UOS) are on the high side, expenses in variable budgets will be higher as well. Therefore, when justifying your expenses over 100%, look at the UOS as well as other possible expenses directly affected by the UOS level. When dealing with revenue, however, it's good to come in over 100%, because it means that you were able to gain more revenue than was budgeted. Such gains often are due to an increase in the number of patients or complexity of those patients.

A lesson in variance analysis

To help you understand and analyze budget variances, let's review figures from the sample cost center report from Chapter 2 (Figure 2.10). The following excerpt is taken from Figure 2.10 and includes analyses explaining each figure.

Salary summary from sample cost center report

Figure 4.1

	Actual	Budget	Variance	%	Prior year
Salaries	$222,156	$191,952	$30,204	(16%)	$198,544

Analysis: The salaries for this month were $30,204 over budget. This equates to a 16% negative variance (30,204 ÷ 191,952 = 0.16). You will need to explain this variance to your supervisor or the committee.

Another way to calculate percentage is: actual ÷ budget = variance
$222,156 ÷ $191,952 = 116%
This shows that you spent 16% more on salaries than the targeted 100%.

First look at the UOS because, as noted earlier, nursing budgets are variable budgets, which means salary expenses increase and decrease depending on UOS. For example, if your unit cared for more patients than were budgeted, you can confidently predict that more money will have been spent on salaries than originally anticipated.

In ancillary areas, ascertain whether your budget is variable or fixed. In some instances, fixed areas are also required to "flex" staff depending on the hospital census. Check your hospital policy. Look at Figure 4.2. Are the UOS higher or lower this month?

UOS summary from sample cost center report

Figure 4.2

	Actual	Budget	Variance	%	Prior year
UOS	625	605	20	3%	645

Analysis: The UOS were 20 more than budgeted for the month, meaning 20 extra patients received care. Does caring for 20 extra patients constitute spending $30,204 extra in salaries? Were the patients very sick? Was there a high acuity? Did staff work a lot of extra shifts, causing the unit to incur a large amount of overtime? As you can see, the UOS variance is only 3% over. This discovery makes it difficult to explain the 16% increase in salary expenses with only a 3% increase in UOS or patient case load (625 ÷ 605 = 103%).

At this point, take a look at the payroll report—an important source document. Typically, you will receive this report twice a month—assuming there are two pay periods. While looking at the payroll report, seek out anything unusual (i.e., did another department code its time to your unit inadvertently?) If you cannot find any discrepancies, pull your admission/discharge/ transfer list for the month. Most units keep this log themselves, but others must obtain it from the admissions or staffing offices. This list contains information such as the number of patients admitted to, transferred into and out of, or discharged from a unit for the entire month.

When reviewing the admission/discharge/transfer list, ask yourself whether the unit had an unexpected number of transfers in or out that were not reflected in the midnight census. Such patients were cared for by staff during the day but were transferred out by midnight, excluding them from the midnight census totals.

Now let's review supplies. See Figure 4.3.

Figure 4.3

Supplies summary from sample cost center report

	Actual	Budget	Variance	%	Prior year
Supplies	$13,222	$12,654	($568)	(4%)	$11,952

Analysis: Even though the unit was over by 20 patients this month, it still managed to go over budget by only $568, or 4%, for supplies. ($13,222 ÷ $12,654 = 104%) This shows good supply management.

Because some hospitals have a "5% rule" that doesn't require managers to explain variance percentages of 5% or under, you may not have to explain that particular line item at all. Ask your supervisor or finance department about the organization's policy.

Let's look at purchased services. Analyze your budget's performance for these services by reviewing the summary in Figure 4.4.

Purchased services summary from sample cost center report

Figure 4.4

Purchased services	Actual	Budget	Variance	%	Prior year
	$85,000	$60,000	($25,000)	(42%)	$54,332

Analysis: As you can see, purchased services are a whopping 42% over budget at $25,000. If this is where outside agency costs are allocated, then the unit is significantly over budget. This is because salaries are already 16% over budget, and now purchased services (another line item that may be dedicated to staff salaries) are 42% over budget. If agency costs are included in purchased services, determine whether the hours worked match up with the dollars paid. In other words, sometimes when agencies are paid, the expense affects the budget in a different month than the one in which the hours were worked. The key is to research to find out. Because purchased services also can include housekeeping or other contracted services, it is important for you to break down this section by what is applicable to HPPD and salary costs. If this line item contains cost for only outside nursing staff, then it will be easier to figure out. If this is the case, combine the percent variance with the regular salary variance to obtain a true picture of the situation ($85,000 ÷ 60,000 = 142%).

To get to the bottom of this huge variance, look over the invoices that were paid for the month. Perhaps a large payment was made covering two months' fees for outside agency or travel nurses, or maybe someone prepaid a bill.

Locate the invoices and begin your analysis. Look for errors that may have caused your unit to be charged incorrectly. For instance, if the purchased services line item does not include nurse registry or nurse travelers, the unit may have been incorrectly charged for the indirect costs that are part of purchased services (i.e., housekeeping or nutritional services). It's important that you find out exactly which services are charged to this line item so you can monitor them accordingly.

'Other' summary from sample cost center report

Figure 4.5

Other	Actual	Budget	Variance	%	Prior year
	$1,500	$600	($900)	(250%)	$720

Analysis: The "other" line item covers expenses such as dues, subscriptions, and outside education. Find out exactly what is charged to this line item, because although the $1,500 actual is a relatively small number compared to the rest of the expenses, a 250% variance stands out greatly.

When building your budget, keep in mind that some costs do not change when volume fluctuates (i.e., subscriptions to monthly nursing journals or professional organization dues) and are divided over the 12-month period.

In this case, it looks as though a staff member attended a conference (perhaps it was prepaid) or dues were paid in a month you hadn't accounted for. Regardless, when you're presenting the budget, your explanation for this variance should echo your analysis of supply management. Also indicate that next month's charges for this line item will be minimal, if any at all.

TIP

Be proactive: Act immediately on your findings rather than waiting to be asked to make improvements. Long before the variance report lands on your desk, you should have a pretty good idea how the numbers you projected for the budget are performing. This is possible by monitoring the unit's financial activity daily.

Once you have reviewed, analyzed, and determined why the numbers were higher or lower than projected, communicate your findings to your boss. He or she may require that you develop and put in place a plan to bring the numbers back in order.

Once you have completed your variance analysis, document your findings to get your budget back on track. Many organizations use specific forms for documenting such information. View the sample variance report in Figure 4.6 below.

Sample variance report

Figure 4.6

Sample variance report

Cost center: _____   Unit: _____
Month: _____   Manager: _____

Item	Actual	Budget	Variance	Explanation	Plan

Productivity reporting

Productivity is how well you are able to control resources when delivering patient care. There are many formulas to determine productivity. However, one of the most popular for healthcare is: **output ÷ input = productivity**

In the nursing department, productivity is measured by using the following formula:
number of hours required ÷ number of hours worked = productivity

For instance, say your weekly nursing productivity is 1,580 hours required or the number of hours necessary to reach 100% productivity based on the budgeted average daily census (ADC) and hours per patient day (HPPD). Also, assume the actual hours worked is 1,780. This shows that, for that week, the nursing department worked an additional 200 hours and was only at 89% productivity (1,580 ÷ 1,780 = 0.89 or 89%).

An example of daily productivity is when 152 hours are required and 160 hours are actually worked. The nursing department worked an additional eight hours, equaling 95% productivity.

Typically, charge or resource nurses are designated to complete the productivity form. By doing this, you allow them to take part in managing the budget while creating ownership. Charge and resource nurses should be well-trained and have good leadership skills to fill this role. These individuals are also responsible for staffing and managing how such resources are used (i.e., the amount of staff used and the skill mix of staff).

After a 24-hour period, the completed productivity form should be given to the nurse manager as well as any written explanations regarding variances in staffing. The charge or resource nurse's documentation should also include any notes regarding activity, sick calls, floating (sending) of staff to or out of the unit, or other unforeseen events.

For the following examples, use an HPPD of 9.5 and a cost of per patient day ($PPD), or CPUOS, of $200 for the direct staff, i.e., registered nurses, licensed practical nurses, and nursing assistants. The nurse manager and monitor technician are indirect staff and are not included in the HPPD. Remember: productivity = output ÷ input.

Sample productivity tool (HPPD only)

Figure 4.7

Unit: _____

Date: _____

	7 a.m.–3 p.m.	3 p.m.–11 p.m.	11 p.m.–7 a.m.
Charge nurse	_____	_____	_____
RNs:	_____	_____	_____
LPNs:	_____	_____	_____
NAs:	_____	_____	_____
Inservice/orientation:	_____	_____	_____
Total:	_____	_____	_____

7 a.m.–3 p.m. total staff: _____

3 p.m.–11 p.m. total staff: _____

11 p.m.–7 a.m. total staff: _____

24 hour total: _____ x 8 hours = _____ hours

Total hours: _____ ÷ midnight census _____ = _____ HPPD

Budgeted HPPD = 9.5

Comments:

Place in the nurse manager's inbox at the end of the night shift each morning.

Completed productivity tool (HPPD only)

Figure 4.8

Unit: Medical-surgical/telemetry

Date: 9/1/08

	7 a.m.–3 p.m.	3 p.m.–11 p.m.	11 p.m.–7 a.m.
Charge nurse	N. Nelson RN	S. Smith RN	J. Jackson RN
RNs:	6	5	4
LPNs:	1	1	0
NAs:	2	1	1
Inservice/orientation:			
Total:	10	7	5

7 a.m.–3 p.m. total staff: _____10_____

3 p.m.–11 p.m. total staff: _____7_____

11 p.m.–7 a.m. total staff: _____5_____

24 hour total:_____22_____ x 8 hours = _____176_____ hours

Total hours:_____176_____ ÷ midnight census_____19_____ = 9.26   HPPD

Budgeted HPPD = 9.5

Comments:
6 patients on telemetry with drips
5 transfers on day shift
Floated K. Kim to 3 West at 3 p.m.
Busy 3 p.m.–11 p.m.
B. Brown IP, orientee 7 a.m.–3 p.m.

Patient classification systems

Patient classification systems assist nurse managers in controlling costs and improving patient care while appropriately using financial resources. Within a nursing unit, patients are ranked at varying acuity levels depending on the complexity of care they require. Patient classification systems are required by various regulatory bodies, including the Centers for Medicare & Medicaid Services' (CMS) Conditions of Participation, The Joint Commission, California's Title 22, and the American Nurses Association's Principles of Staffing. Check with your state to determine its specific requirements.

To measure the care needed for each patient, hospitals often assign a certain number of HPPD figures for each acuity level. Along with these acuity measurements come whole systems for classifying patients' complexity levels. Some of these systems are extremely intricate, while others are quite simple. Such systems may be computerized, off-the-shelf programs or created specifically for the needs of the hospital. Regardless of the sophistication of these programs, the more complex or ill the patient is, the more nursing resources they require.

For the medical-surgical/telemetry unit and HPPD of 9.5, assume the noncomplex patients require less nursing care hours than more complex patients. As you may recall, when we built the budget, we calculated for a percentage of patients to be at the medical-surgical level and another percentage to be at the telemetry level in Figure 3.2. The reason for this is that we cannot determine the patient's acuity level until he or she is admitted and assessed. Looking back at the breakdown in Figure 3.2, 53% of our budgeted patients will be in the medical-surgical category (level 1), while the remaining 47% will be in the telemetry category (level 2).

Although the level 1 and 2 categories are used to guide you in assessing what types of patients your department will care for, you must use your unit-specific patient classification system to accurately assess the level of care required for each patient. In fact, when planning the budget, take patients' acuity levels into consideration so you can predict the patients' care needs. For example, a patient awaiting discharge will require less hours of care than a patient with multiple intravenous lines or limited mobility or who is dependent on complex procedures. Also use your patient classification system to monitor staffing and productivity. This is important because hospitals often staff by census, availability, or upon the requests of the charge nurse from the previous shift, which can put patients' safety at risk. Another risky staffing practice is assigning a nurse—no matter what his or her competency level—to a certain area rather than basing workloads on patient acuity levels and staff competence.

Performing a breakeven analysis

Once you determine the budgeted ADC (see Step #2 in Chapter 3), make sure maintaining this census is both profitable and safe. In Chapter 3, it was determined that the unit would run an ADC of 20.55. Now let's see if this is a financially appropriate census. There are minimum staffing levels for each unit. These levels are based on the following:

- State laws that define ratios for the number of patients per nurse

- Hospital policies

- Break and lunch coverage (i.e., who watches patients when the nurse caring for them is on a break or away at lunch)

- Unit logistics (i.e., the ability to watch all patients, which may require additional staff)

- Transfer unit activity (e.g., if there is a low census on the unit but you anticipate many admissions from other units, you may need to staff two nurses to prepare for the incoming patients).

The breakeven analysis helps you determine whether it's financially feasible to keep the unit open. Consider both direct and indirect costs. That's because the bill for indirect costs such as electricity, copy machines, fax lines, and phones must still be paid even if the unit is at low census or closed. It's up to you to know at what point or dollar amount the hospital begins to lose money on direct and indirect costs. Ask your finance department about such figures, because you must also articulate them to your supervisor and the committee.

To determine the unit breakeven census point, determine the minimum staff necessary per shift (Strasen 1987). As an example, use the information listed in Figure 4.9. For the example, assume the hospital's policy is to staff monitor technicians 24 hours a day, seven days a week regardless of census. Also assume that the nurse manager is not "flexed," or taken off, the unit. In other words, he or she works on the unit 40 hours a week and the hours are spread out over seven days. In instances in which the unit is closed for long periods, the manager's hours stay the same as he or she will likely be assigned to take on additional duties, such as managing other units.

Figure 4.9

Medical-surgical/telemetry unit
Minimum hours ÷ HPPD = breakeven point

Shift	RNs	Monitor technicians	Hours
7 a.m.–3 p.m.	2	1	24
3 p.m.–11 p.m.	2	1	24
11 p.m.–7 p.m.	2	1	24
Nurse manager	(40 hours ÷ 7 days)		5.7
Total hours			**77.7**

Minimum hours ÷ HPPD = breakeven point
77.7 ÷ 9.5 = **8.17 patients**

The telemetry unit must maintain a minimum ADC of 8.17 patients to cover the direct costs of staffing for the unit. If the census drops below 8.17, the unit will incur higher costs than are allotted for the HPPD of 9.5. For instance, if only seven patients are cared for, the HPPD would be 11.1 (77.7 ÷ 7 = 11.1).

Cutting a budget

There are times when you must reevaluate or cut your budget mid-year. Unforeseen circumstances, such as the loss of key insurance contracts, heightened competition, or low census, lead to this necessary reevaluation. In fact, if the census remains below budget for any length of time, the administrative team may ask all departments to cut costs, consolidate patients, and close units, or they may mandate an organizationwide cut. In such cases, hospital administration may begin enforcing a mandatory paid time off policy, or its members may try to set an example by taking days off without pay. Other measures to address unforeseen circumstances include a "no overtime" policy, a temporary cease in hiring, consolidating positions, or, in some instances, layoffs.

Other controllable costs

Poor performers, dissatisfied staff, and turnover

Cost containment is not just about salaries and supply expenses. Monitoring staff's performance is equally important. Because the cost of poor performance is difficult to quantify, it must be taken seriously and kept under control with good management and leadership. Negativity, such as poor performance, turnover, and an unsatisfactory unit environment, weighs heavily on the budget. Considering the bulk of your budget is spent on personnel, it's imperative that you understand the effect such problems can have.

Unhappy or inadequately trained nurses can result in increased turnover and cause costly errors. It's for these reasons that you must provide each staff member the opportunity to learn and grow within the organization. The more satisfied nurses are, the longer they will stay employed with your hospital.

Although many people think unsatisfactory salaries drive nurses out of hospitals, other factors—such as professional treatment and positive work environment—consistently rate higher for employee satisfaction. As a manager, you must maintain open communication, be available to staff, and listen to their concerns—these are the core managerial skills that aid in staff retention. Practice of such skills may seem a lot to ask from a busy manager who has to worry about the unit's financials. However, keep in mind that one nurse can cost up to $75,000 to replace. Can your budget afford that?

Another of your responsibilities is counseling, and sometimes terminating, poor performers. In essence, you are the chief retention officer on your unit. In this role, decide the best approach for handling problem employees. You may have to face difficult decisions, such as firing a problem employee or deciding to counsel him or her and taking the risk of losing five other employees by keeping the problem employee on. Think about these dilemmas and how they affect both the budget and productivity.

Above all, talk with your staff. By regularly communicating with staff, you're more likely to learn about problems, such as disruptive physicians, inappropriate staffing, lack of supplies, and other work environment dilemmas, before they become large issues. When you learn of such problems, you then have an obligation to resolve them. If you don't talk with staff or attempt to improve such problems, your nurses will leave.

Patient care and staff education

Another area that requires constant monitoring is the quality of patient care. The cost of poor care can be expensive—and deadly. Medication errors and decubitis ulcers result in lengthened patient stays and increased costs. Remember in Chapter 1, we discussed the new CMS reimbursement guidelines for certain preventable conditions. Mistakes can be extremely costly.

To ensure that staff members are properly trained and can give the highest-quality care possible to your patients, offer them regular training to keep them up to date on the latest care techniques. Remember to budget for the education hours offered on your unit.

Orientation

Orientation costs can be significant, so control them whenever possible. If a clinical nurse specialist/staff educator is not the person in charge of orientation, evaluate the average length of the program. For instance, evaluate the performance of new hires at 30 and 90 days, then decide whether they are competent to care for the patients on your unit. Managers often extend orientation time, thinking that the longer a nurse is trained the better. This is not necessarily the case. Instead, use orientation as a probation period to weed out poor performers.

It's important that you budget adequate dollars for orientation, because no nurse should be pulled off orientation prematurely to fill a staffing hole. Although it does occur, this risky practice not only jeopardizes the safety of patients but also affects the new nurse, as he or she may not be prepared to provide care alone.

BONUS TOOLS

For a list of six questions to keep in mind when budgeting for orientation, education, and training, look in the Chapter 4 folder on this book's accompanying CD-ROM.

Annual performance reviews

The annual performance review is an evaluation of the staff's performance for the entire year. Just as you must closely manage the budget to evaluate its performance, you also must monitor your staff. By watching staff perform their jobs daily and consistently communicating with them, you will use the annual performance reviews most effectively.

To make the most of performance reviews, allow ample time for discussion—after all, you are talking to a person about the job he or she does every day and your opinion of the quality o that work. This is a meaningful process to staff and often one of the few times they get your undivided attention.

When going over performance reviews with staff, ask them for feedback about your performance—ask them whether you meet their needs. Also, ask staff for at least one suggestion regarding performance improvement on the unit. By doing this, you give them a safe outlet for expressing any concerns they may have. Be sure to allow time to review last year's goals and, later, work on the new goals together.

From a financial perspective, annual performance reviews may lead to increased salaries, as many hospitals base staff raises on performance. Other organizations may base raises on years of service or the staff's level of clinical expertise. Either way, every hospital allots a certain amount each year for salary increases. Find out what salary percentages your hospital is offering its staff, as the amount may change from year to year.

Chapter 5

BUILDING A BUSINESS CASE

Learning objectives

After reading this chapter, the learner will be able to:

- Identify the process to construct a business plan
- Explain return on investment
- Describe return on investment's importance to cost/benefit analysis

Reevaluating your plan

Sometimes, after you have begun implementing the budget, circumstances arise that require you to reevaluate your unit's financial plan. Such circumstances may include the following:

- **Sustained high census.** For instance, say your budgeted average daily census is 20.55, but for the last 90 days, census has remained consistently at 26, requiring you to use travel nurses, overtime, and agency staff.

- **Change in physician practices.** For example, if a physician who frequents your unit acquires a new skill, his or her patients may require additional hours of care. Also, staff may require additional training to accommodate the needs of such patients.

- **Offering additional services.** Occasionally, your hospital may need to offer a new service, such as outpatient care, to stay competitive. Say a physician makes appointments with his patients two days after discharge for follow-up outpatient care. He is forced to use the clinic across the street because your hospital doesn't offer such services, even though your unit has unused space perfect for performing such procedures.

- **Restructuring physical logistics.** Changing of physical logistics such as mid-year layout changes to accommodate another office, patient room, kitchen, or other renovations over $25,000 can alter your budget. (Ask your supervisor about the amount of money necessary for building a plan, but know that plans are usually for big-ticket items rather than smaller projects such as moving a nursing workstation to a new location.)

- **Need for a clinical educator.** You may want to hire a clinical educator to work with new staff to increase competency. Such a need is unit-specific and must be well-justified.

- **Need for an additional full-time equivalent (FTE).** If there are significant changes in volume, admissions, acuity, or other factors, you may need another staff member. Although the "budget is the budget," you may need to make a case for additional FTE. If so, presenting the business case clearly and effectively is important.

Regardless of the circumstance, you must know how to request additional services, staff, or funds. In some organizations, the annual budgeting process also involves developing a comprehensive business plan for the next year or for a prescribed period (i.e., a three-year plan aligned with the hospital's strategic plan) (Barnum and Kerfoot 1995). In this chapter, we will discuss how to write a business plan, propose a formal business case, and present it to administration in a confident and professional way.

Business planning

A business plan is a written document that summarizes a business opportunity. It outlines what the management team can expect to gain and the steps it must follow to take advantage of the opportunity (Timmons 1994). Business plans are tools and thus must be comprehensive. They also call your target audience to action. In the business world, for example, such proposals or plans are often written by outside vendors to persuade a particular company to do business with the vendor.

You may have an idea or want to try something different for improving efficiency on your unit, and if the request is large enough, you might find yourself required to prepare and present a business case to your supervisor. The case to your supervisor may be brief, perhaps only one or two pages long. If approved, he or she may ask that you formally draft a business plan with the information you presented.

A good way to test the waters when seeking to make large changes within your unit or the organization is by using pilot testing. Consider presenting a business case for a pilot project instead of making large, unfounded requests. Pilot projects act as testing grounds for system or procedural changes. Such projects must have definite start and finish dates to allow evaluation at the end.

Following the project's evaluation—assuming it was successful and you plan to take it further—you must write a formal business plan.

Because the terms "business plan," "business case," and "proposal" are sometimes used interchangeably, it's important to find out what the process is called in your organization and how it works. For example, some hospitals have a formal process and proposal template for preparing a business plan. Throughout this chapter, we will review the basic concepts for writing a business plan. These concepts can be modified to best suit your facility's protocol.

You may be asked to write a business plan if you are responsible for:

- Reviewing specific business opportunities.
- Responding to census changes by requesting additional staff.
- Purchasing equipment for your area.

Once you identify the need for a new service or piece of equipment, write a professional business plan to present to senior leadership. Regardless of whether it's required in your hospital, writing such plans or proposals is a good skill to have. Also, the plan or proposal will serve as an outline for your argument when you are requesting funding for unplanned expenses.

Twelve key components of a business plan

There are various guidelines for business plans; many are listed in steps, many by sections. Although each facility may list them in a different order, the following components are a necessary part of every business plan:

1. Executive summary

Every business plan begins with a brief executive summary. This summary introduces the key components of a business plan. It allows busy executives who review many business plans a day to quickly glance over the plan's initiative. The length of the executive summary varies greatly depending on what you present. If you are presenting a business case, it may be two paragraphs long. An executive summary for a business plan—which is a detailed plan—may be closer to two pages in length.

Use the executive summary to describe the project's importance, the problem or issue it addresses, and how it fulfills the hospital's overall goals. When writing this section, consider your audience and write directly for them. Do they know about the current situation on the unit that leads you to seek change? If your audience knows nothing of the situation, first explain the problem and then give any necessary additional information.

TIP

When writing the executive summary—or any presentation for that matter—learn who your audience is before you begin. Be sure to mold the presentation to your audience's needs and desires. If you are speaking to the chief executive officer, make sure your presentation solves a problem that directly affects the hospital's bottom line or addresses specific regulations such as those mandated by The Joint Commission or the state.

Other things to factor into your presentation are relativity and timing. In other words, if your hospital chose to close its obstetrics business, then writing a business plan for an obstetrics clinic would be a waste of everyone's time, plus you'd seem uninformed about the hospital. Timing also is important. For example, if you are requesting money, be sure your request does not follow closely on the heels of layoffs or after the executives have just revealed less than satisfactory financial statements to staff.

---

2. Description of the present situation and summary of existing conditions

Your description of the present situation should be a main focus of the business plan. This, of course, is because it explains the immediate need for the project/product. Be brief and concise when explaining the existing conditions. Administrative team members sit through many presentations, and they will appreciate your thorough yet to-the-point explanation of the issue and your proposed solution.

Review the following sample description and summary to get an understanding of how to present an issue in the business proposal:

> *Because of the increase of short-stay patients on the unit during the week, activity on the unit has increased, rendering the current staffing patterns inadequate for the growth in volume. Also, these high-acuity patients are not reflected in our midnight census. Therefore, our productivity appears low yet we are not meeting our budget.*

3. Description of the new program/proposed solution

Use this section of the business proposal to offer your solution for the problem you just presented. Describe the procedure or equipment that you're requesting, which staff it will help or affect, and any procedural or budgetary changes it will impact.

Review the following sample description:

> *Hiring an additional 1.0 FTE of an RN will enable the unit to care for these short-stay patients in a more cost-effective, timely manner. This RN will also serve as the liaison to the physicians, staff, patients, and family members. He or she will be the point person for orders and questions.*

4. Development of goals and objectives

A goal is a broad statement of a desired outcome. Each hospital has its own set of goals prepared by administration using input from all levels of management. When writing your goals, be sure they are:

- Aligned with the organization's mission statement, vision, or values
- Broad-based
- Achievable and realistic
- Challenging
- Result-oriented

Example of a goal: Become the leader of cardiac care in the tri-county area.

Objectives are specific statements detailing the measures necessary to achieve the desired out-come. When writing your objectives, be sure they:

- Start with "to" and are followed by an action verb
- Outline a single result
- Have a specific time frame and completion date
- Are realistic and attainable
- Are consistent with the resources that are or will be available

Example of an objective: To develop and implement a comprehensive cardiac rehabilitation program by fall of 2006, located on the second floor, which will be operated by trained staff and managed by the director of cardiology.

Let's say that for the medical-surgical/telemetry unit we're managing, we have identified the need for an additional staff nurse because of increased activity within the past three months. Unit staff are caring for the increased census, which includes a high number of short-stay pa-tients. Such patients do not count toward midnight census because they are discharged before midnight. Therefore, the unit does not receive revenue from the outpatients and must pay the staff-related expenses for their care. In this case, your objective might be:

> *To hire a full-time RN to act as an admissions/transfer/discharge nurse who meets the needs of our short-stay patients and our increased activity and to establish a separate cost center to track revenue and expenses.*

5. Presentation of options

In this section of the business proposal, review all possible options for handling the situation presented earlier. By doing so, you allow those making the decision to weigh all of the possible outcomes and make an informed decision. Address the following three options when present-ing this section:

Option #1: Keep the status quo and do nothing. When stating the first option, fully explain the ramifications of allowing the project/product to remain the same. For example, you might say to the committee:

If we do not take care of the problem now, overtime expenses will continue to rise. Therefore, until we develop a mechanism accounting for the increased activity, we will continue to incur overtime.

Option #2: The proposed solution. Use this option to address anticipated costs and share with the decision-makers the results you expect to see. Be sure to tell the committee specifically, with set dates, when you expect to start working on the project or to purchase equipment. For instance, you might tell the committee your proposed solution is to:

Hire an additional 1.0 FTE RN by November 1, 2008, to act as cardiac admissions/ transfer/discharge nurse and patient educator. The RN's responsibilities include overseeing the admission/transfer process, patient education as it relates to discharge instructions, and the discharge itself. Develop a new cost center for all revenues for short-stay patients and related staff and supplies expenses.

Option #3: Secondary solutions. If you have a secondary solution or back-up plan you would like to introduce, now is the time to do so. Because it's your second proposed solution, fully explain why it's not your first option and why you feel your original solution is better. Do this by listing the pros and cons of each. For example, you might tell the committee that your secondary solution is to:

Designate exclusive space and staff to care for short-stay patients rather than absorbing them into the unit. This calls for a complete business plan with a cost/benefit analysis, which most likely would not be completed solely by the nurse manager, as it would include other stakeholders and involve further analysis.

6. Cost/benefit analysis

This section identifies what you are asking for in terms of money/labor. For extensive projects or equipment, you may have to develop a timeline that shows upfront costs, monthly costs/expenses, and when revenues will offset the expenses. This must also show stakeholders when the project will become profitable or when the return on investment (ROI) is expected to occur. The ROI is an important part of the analysis, particularly for the finance committee or administration. They'll want see whether this project/product will pay for itself within six months, two years, etc. Prepare such statements for a three- to four-year time period or until breakeven occurs. Breakeven is when revenues and expenses are the same, or when the project/product pays for itself. The faster you can show the breakeven point, the more likely your idea will be approved.

Within this section, you are expected to quantify the amount of money/labor needed for the new procedure or equipment. For example, your cost/benefit analysis might read:

1.0 (FTE) x 2,080 (number of paid hours per year) x $30 (average pay rate for RNs) = $62,400 per year. The new position does not require replacement because it is a Monday–Friday position. However, there are costs related to benefits; benefits are at 30%. The total salary expense equals $81,120.

Overtime expenses for last month were $5,400. Much of this is directly attributed to the additional staff needed to care for the short-stay patients. After implementing the new RN position, we expect this amount to decrease by 75%, creating a $48,600 savings anticipated by the third month of the project. As noted earlier, short-stay patient revenue is not being allocated to the unit cost center. It is recommended that a separate cost center be developed to track both revenue and expenses. The overall impact of this would be an increase in FTEs. However, it would be designated to the appropriate cost center and justified by the revenue from more lucrative outpatient procedures.

7. Market analysis

Use this section to explain why external market forces will help lead to the program's success. This section is optional, depending on your request. If you are requesting an additional FTE, this may not be necessary. For extensive business plans, this includes a SWOT (strengths, weaknesses, opportunities, and threats) analysis. Also include in this section the data you gathered to back your claims. Such data could include your admission/discharge/transfer data, projected cardiac catheterizations volume for the next six months, physician practice patterns, and so on. As an example, you might present the following to the committee:

Over the last six months, admissions for short-stay patients have increased by 25%. The unit receives an average of five short-stay patient transfers or admissions per day, which was not anticipated during the budget process. These patients are discharged before midnight and are not counted in the midnight census. After surveying other area hospitals, we have identified the best practice. We found that most hospitals designate specific areas to care for these patients. Other hospitals also assign cost centers for revenue and expenses, which the current nurse manager must manage.

8. Explanation of program/product and its implementation

Now it's time to explain how you or your staff will put the new program/product into practice. Introduce a communication plan, which is a written plan explaining the method you will use to communicate all related changes to the stakeholders. This is done via a formal memorandum, by verbally explaining the project during staff meetings, or by sending out weekly e-mail updates about the project's progress. For example, you might share the following implementation plan with the committee:

We will develop the job description and determine the salary structure, and Human Resources will then post the position internally. We will accept résumés for 72 hours after the posting. Following, the manager will interview candidates with charge nurses from each shift. The top two candidates will be selected to interview with the physicians, nurse manager, and clinical nurse specialist. We then will make an offer to the most qualified individual, and upon acceptance, we will set the start date according to the unit schedule. (If the person hired is an internal staff member, we will make every effort to replace his or her position immediately.)

We will hold a mandatory staff meeting explaining the new position and its associated roles and responsibilities. We will also revise staffing schedules to include the position. Working with the finance department, we will establish a cost center number and a name for the area (e.g., short-stay unit or 3 West, short-stay). By working with the admissions office, we will develop a communication plan to ensure that patients are coded appropriately.

9. Timeline and schedule for implementation

Develop and insert a clear, realistic timeline in this section. Remember to take into consideration budget cycle, pay periods, holiday time, etc., because they affect the amount of time people can afford to spend working on the project.

BONUS TOOLS

To review a sample timeline, look in the Chapter 5 folder of your CD-ROM.

10. Description of program/product leader and summary of required resources

In this section of the proposal, state who will be responsible for implementing the new program/product. If you will be the leader and point person for the effort, state that. Name others who will have responsibility, such as charge nurses, the staffing office, and physicians. For example, the description might read:

> *Responsible persons: manager, charge nurses, physician director, staffing office, admissions office.*

11. Evaluation of program

The committee or your supervisor will want to know how the program/product is working and when you will evaluate its progress. Perhaps you plan to use productivity data to track the success of the program/product. Employee, physician, and patient satisfaction surveys are also great ways to monitor and evaluate progress.

As the presenter, it's up to you to set the evaluation date. Will the evaluation program begin in 90 days, six months, etc.? Examples of both when and how the evaluation process will be handled might be described as follows:

> *The program will be evaluated at 90 days and again at six months. The following will be used:*

> • *Productivity and overtime reports*
> • *New cost center monthly financial report*

- *Patient, physician, charge nurse, and other staff satisfaction surveys*
- *Length of stay*

12. Financial presentation

The financial presentation is the final component of the business plan. This is where you outline the bottom line and tell your audience how much the proposed solution will cost. In fact, you will notice many executives like to page through to this section right away to view the bottom line numbers. Because it is of such great importance to your audience, it is imperative that you have a clear depiction of this bottom line and pay off, or ROI. ROI is what the hospital can expect to gain from funding the proposed program/product (in this case, for the new RN position).

TIP

When preparing your financial presentation, keep it to one page. Remember: Your audience includes executives who are busy and look at many reports each day. Keep it short and to the point—the bottom line.

An example of the financial presentation might go as follows:

1.0 FTE x 2,080 x $30 = $62,400 per year. The new position does not require replacement because it is a Monday–Friday position. However, there are costs related to benefits; benefits are at 30%. The total salary expense equals $81,120.

Currently, overtime expenses for last month were $5,400. Much of this is directly attributed to the additional staff needed to care for the short-stay patients. By implementing the new RN position, we expect this amount to decrease by 75%, creating a $48,600 savings. However, some incremental overtime will exist.

Revenue from short-stay patients is currently being allocated to surgical services and is difficult to quantify. After working with the accounts receivable department and analyzing the list of short-stay patients over the last 90 days, we determined that we are receiving approximately $1,100 per patient in reimbursement.

We anticipate that with an ADC of five patients x five days a week x 50 weeks (no surgeries scheduled during holidays) = 1,250 patients per year. Anticipated revenue *of $1,100 per patient x1,250 patients = $1,375,000*

Revenue: $1,375,000

Less expenses: $81,120 (new position)

$2,500 (supplies)

Profit/net income: $1,291,380

This is a high-level projection/budget. If the proposal is approved, a complete budget will be developed adding indirect costs.

Preparation is key

Preparation is the first step in writing a business plan. To properly prepare, you must talk to stakeholders and collect data. In this case, speak to the surgery manager, physicians, and accounting department staff or whoever is in charge of revenue allocation. Also, speak with the admissions office, because they will ensure that short-stay admissions are coded to the new cost center, the staffing office so they understand which staff belong on each unit now that you manage two cost centers, and your supervisor.

Collecting historical data for the defined time period is also crucial for getting your business proposal approved. For instance, use the productivity tool (Figure 4.7) in Chapter 4 to help build your case. Future projections are also necessary, as they allow decision-makers a clear view of the program/product's value in the grand scheme of the hospital's operation. Make appointments with the departments affected by the change (i.e., admitting or accounting, in our example) so you can collect your data and get their buy-in and support. Never submit a plan without first having the support of affected departments/physicians. Inform any department, in detail, that will be affected.

Conclusion

As mentioned earlier in the book, whether for-profit or not-for-profit, hospitals are businesses. And hospital managers are expected to have skills similar to those who work in other industries. Such skills include proposal writing, business planning, and finance and budgeting. Another skill that is critical—and perhaps is most important—to your success as a manager is the ability to converse at a professional level about the issues on your unit. You must be able to think critically about such issues and present and discuss well-thought-out solutions.

Figure 5.1 is an example of a short, concise business plan following the 12 steps indicated in Chapter 5. Depending on the proposal or project, some of the steps may be consolidated, others may be expanded. Use this sample as a guide.

Figure 5.1

Executive summary

As the hospital's patient population is shifting more toward outpatient care, the number of short-stay patients is increasing. Short-stay patients are those that stay in the hospital for 23 hours or less and are then discharged to home. These patients are placed on the inpatient surgical units for care and are not included in the midnight census.

After collecting data for a six-month period, it is evident that 5 West's productivity has been affected due to this unplanned volume of patients.

Description of the present situation

Because of an increase in the number of short-stay patients on the unit during the week, activity on the unit has increased, rendering the current staffing patterns inadequate for this growth in volume. Also, these high-acuity patients are not reflected in the midnight census. As our unit "absorbs" these patients to provide care, the staff salaries continue to be allocated to the med-surg cost center, which increases our cost per patient day.

Proposed solution

Hiring an additional 1.0 RN FTE will enable the unit to care for these short-stay patients in a more cost-effective, timely manner. This RN will also serve as the liaison to physicians, staff, and family members. He or she will be the point person for physician orders and questions that may arise.

Goal

Provide safe, cost-effective care for med-surg and short-stay patients.

Objectives

1. To hire a full-time RN to act as an admissions/transfer/discharge (ADT) nurse who meets the needs of our short-stay patients and our increased activity
2. To establish a separate cost center to track the revenue and expenses associated with short-stay patients

Option #1
Do nothing and continue staffing as we have. If we do not address this problem soon, overtime expenses will continue to rise. Staff satisfaction has been affected and we are at risk of losing key staff members. Therefore, until we develop a mechanism to account for the increased activity, we will continue to incur overtime and continue to use traveling nurses.

Option #2
Hire an additional 1.0 RN FTE by November 2008. This RN will act as an ADT nurse on the med-surg unit. The RN's responsibilities will include overseeing the ADT process, providing patient education as it relates to discharge instructions, and facilitating the discharge itself.

Develop a new cost center to address the revenue associated with short-stay patients and the expenses associated with nurses' salaries, supplies, linen, equipment, food, and other items. The current nurse manager of the med-surg unit will manage this cost center.

Option #3
Designate exclusive space in the hospital to staff and care for the short-stay patients rather than "absorbing" them on the inpatient unit. This option would call for a complete business plan with a cost/benefit analysis, which most likely would not be completed solely by the nurse manager, as it would include other stakeholders such as engineering, finance, and other departments.

Sample business plan for a medical-surgical unit (cont.)

Figure 5.1

Cost/benefit analysis

This new position will not need a replacement component because it is a Monday–Friday position. A 1.0 (FTE) x 2,080 (number of paid hours per year) x $30 (average hourly pay rate for RNs) = $62,400 per year. Benefits are currently running 30% (according to human resources [HR]), for a total salary of $81,120.

Overtime expenses were $5,400 last month on the med-surg unit. Much of this is directly attributed to the additional staff needed to care for the short-stay patients. After implementing the new RN position, we expect this amount to decrease by 75%, creating a savings of $48,600 anticipated by the third month of the project. As noted earlier, short-stay-patient revenue is not being allocated to the unit cost center. It is recommended that a separate cost center be developed to track both revenue and expenses. The overall effect of this change would be an increase in FTEs by 1.0. However, it would be designated to the appropriate cost center and justified by the revenue from more lucrative outpatient procedures.

Market analysis

Over the past six months, admissions for short-stay patients have increased by 25%. The med-surg unit receives an average of five short-stay patient transfers or admissions per day, which was not anticipated during the budget process. These patients are discharged before midnight and are not counted in the midnight census. After surveying other area hospitals and reviewing articles in journals regarding this topic, we have identified a best practice. We found that many hospitals designate specific areas in the hospital to care for these patients, particularly those hospitals with high volume. Other hospitals also assign cost centers to monitor revenue and expenses, which the current nurse manager manages.

Explanation of the program and its implementation

We will develop a job description for the RN position and determine the salary structure, working with HR. HR will post the new job internally prior to posting it in the local newspaper. We will accept applications and resumes for 72 hours after the position has been posted. If no resumes or no qualified applications are received, we will then advertise in the local newspaper.

Once qualified applicants have been identified, the nurse manager and the charge nurses from each shift will interview the candidates. The top two candidates will be selected to interview with two key physicians, the nurse manager, and the clinical nurse specialist on the unit. We will then select and make an offer to the most qualified individual, and upon acceptance, we will set the start date according to the unit schedule. (If the person hired is an internal staff member, we will make every effort to replace his or her position immediately, working closely with that nurse manager and HR.)

We will hold a mandatory staff meeting explaining the new position and its associated roles and responsibilities. We will also update the staffing schedules to reflect the new position. Working with the finance department, we will establish a cost center number and a name for the area (e.g., short-stay unit or 3 West, short-stay). By working with the admissions office, we will develop a communication plan to ensure that patients are coded appropriately. Additionally, we will develop a communication memo to all staff members regarding how to code their time on their time cards if they care for the short-stay patients.

Timeline and schedule for implementation

September 1–15: Develop job description
September 15–17: Post job internally
September 17–25: Accept applications
September 25–October 14: Conduct interviews
October 14–16: Make offer
October 16–20: Meet with finance to secure cost center
October 20–22: Meet with admissions to review coding
November 2: Begin project with RN scheduled Monday–Friday

| Figure 5.1 | **Sample business plan for a medical-surgical unit (cont.)** |

Description of program leader and resources needed

Responsible persons include the following:

- Lead: Nurse manager
- Team: Charge nurses from all three shifts:

  - Physicians (Dr. X and Dr. Y)
  - Staffing office
  - Admissions office
  - Finance office
  - Recovery room staff

Evaluation of program

The program will be evaluated in 90 days and again at six months following the start of the program. The following reports will be used:

- Productivity reports
- Overtime reports
- New cost center monthly financial reports
- Patient, physician, charge nurse, and staff satisfaction surveys
- Length of stay on med-surg unit

Financial

1.0 FTE x 2,080 x $30 = $62,400 per year. The new position does not require replacement because it is a Monday–Friday position. However, there are costs related to benefits; benefits are at 30%. The total salary expense equals $81,120.

Currently, overtime expenses for last month were $5,400. Much of this is directly attributed to the additional staff needed to care for the short-stay patients. By implementing the new RN position, we expect this amount to decrease by 75%, creating a $48,600 savings. However, some incremental overtime will exist.

Revenue from short-stay patients is currently being allocated to surgical services and is difficult to quantify. After working with the accounts receivable department and analyzing the list of short-stay patients over the past 90 days, we determined that we are receiving approximately $1,100 per patient in reimbursement.

We anticipate that with an ADC of five patients x five days per week x 50 weeks (no surgeries scheduled during holidays) = 1,250 patients per year. Anticipated revenue of $1,100 per patient x 1,250 patients = $1,375,000.

Revenue:	$1,375,000
Less expenses:	81,120 (new position)
	2,500 (supplies)
Profit/net income:	**$1,291,380**

This is a high-level projection/budget. If the proposal is approved, a complete budget will be created that will include indirect costs.

REFERENCES

Barnum, B. and Kerfoot, K. M. (1995). *The Nurse as Executive, Fourth Edition*. New York: Aspen Publishers, Inc.

Brock, S. L. (1992). Writing Business Proposals and Reports: Key Strategies for Success. (Fifty Minute Series.) Menlo Park, CA: Crisp Publications.

Centers for Medicare and Medicaid Services. (2007). Information retrieved from *www.cms.hhs.gov.*

Finkler, S. and Kovner, C. T. (2000). *Financial Management for Nurse Managers and Executives, Second Edition*. Philadelphia: W.B. Saunders.

Huber, D. (2005). *Leadership and Nursing Care Management, Third Edition*. Philadelphia: W.B. Saunders.

Johnson, J. E. (1990). "Developing an effective business plan." *Nursing Economic$* 8: 152-154.

Labor Management Institute (LMI) (2007). *Labor Management Institute Best Practices Position Control*. Bloomington, MN = CMI.

Livingstone, J. (2001). *The Portable MBA in Finance and Accounting, Third Edition.* New York: John Wiley and Sons.

Marelli, T.M. (2004). *The Nurse Manager's Survival Guide, Third Edition.* St. Louis: Mosby. National Coalition on Health Care. (2007). "Health insurance cost." Available at *www.nchc.org.*

Strasen, L. (1987). *Key Business Skills for Nurse Managers.* Philadelphia: Lippincott Williams & Wilkins.

Timmons, J.A. (1994). *New Venture Creation: Entrepreneurship in the 21st Century, Fourth Edition.* Columbus, OH: McGraw Hill College.

United States Census Bureau. (2007). "Household income rises, poverty rate declines, number of uninsured up." Available at *www.census.gov.*

Vestal, K. W. (1988). "Writing a Business Plan." *Nursing Economic$* 6: 121-124.

- Discuss the foreign language of finance
- Identify the components of a financial statement
- Explain the differences between a balance sheet and income and departmental expenditures
- Describe the process of budgeting for staff, supplies, equipment, and capital expenditures
- Identify the process to construct a budget
- Describe breakdown analysis
- Define controllable costs
- Explain how to manage controllable costs
- Identify the process to construct a business plan
- Explain return on investment
- Describe return on investment's importance to cost/benefit analysis

Faculty

KT Waxman, DNP, MBA, RN, CNL, has more than 20 years of experience as a nurse leader. She is currently the president and chief nursing officer for KT Waxman and Associates, her healthcare consulting firm in the East Bay area of California.

Accreditation/Designation statement

HCPro is accredited as a provider of continuing nursing education by the American Nurses Credentialing Center Commission on Accreditation.

This educational activity for 3 nursing contact hours is provided by HCPro, Inc.

Disclosure statements

HCPro, Inc. has a conflict of interest policy that requires course faculty to disclose any real or apparent commercial financial affiliations related to the content of their presentations/materials. It is not assumed that these financial interests or affiliations will have an adverse impact on faculty presentations; they are simply noted here to fully inform the participants.

KT Waxman has declared that she has no commercial/financial vested interest in this activity.

Instructions

In order to be eligible to receive your nursing contact hours for this activity, you are required to do the following:

1. Read the book, *A Practical Guide to Finance and Budgeting, Second Edition*
2. Complete the exam
3. Complete the evaluation
4. Provide your contact information on the exam and evaluation
5. Submit exam and evaluation to HCPro, Inc.

Please provide all of the information requested above and mail or fax your completed exam, program evaluation, and contact information to

>HCPro, Inc.
>Attention: Continuing Education Manager
>75 Sylvan Street, Suite A-101
>Danvers, MA 01923
>Fax: 781/639-2982

NOTE:

This book and associated exam are intended for individual use only. If you would like to provide this continuing education exam to other members of your nursing staff, please contact our customer service department at 877/727-1728 to place your order. The exam fee schedule is as follows:

Exam quantity	Fee
1	$0
2–25	$15 per person
26–50	$12 per person
51–100	$8 per person
101+	$5 per person

Continuing education exam

Name: _____

Title: _____

Facility name: _____

Address: _____

Address: _____

City: _____ State: _____ ZIP: _____

Phone number: _____ Fax number: _____

E-mail: _____

Nursing license number: _____

(ANCC requires a unique identifier for each learner)

1. **There is a revenue cycle in each hospital that dictates how money flows throughout the organization. At what point in the cycle are employee salaries, supplies, and medications paid?**

   a. They are paid directly after the patient is admitted to the hospital.

   b. They are paid directly before the payment is collected.

   c. They are paid directly after contractual allowances have been deducted.

   d. They are paid directly before contractual allowances have been deducted.

2. **Acronyms are a large part of the foreign language of finance. What does the acronym FTE represent?**

   a. The total cost of salaries divided by the units of service.

   b. The number of hours divided by the number of patient days.

   c. The specific item the organization produces and delivers to its customers.

   d. The equivalent of one full-time employee working for one year.

3. **What does the acronym HPPD represent?**

   a. Hours per patient day

   b. Hours per pertinent department

   c. Hours per patient discharge

   d. Hourly payment per director

4. **"Contractual allowances" is an item on the balance sheet. What does this term refer to?**

    a.   The amount of money the hospital budgets for free care.

    b.   The difference between the amount of money the hospital bills third-party payers and the amount the hospital actually receives for reimbursement.

    c.   All of the charges made to insurance companies and patients for outstanding payments for a particular time period.

    d.   The assets that the patient or insurer is responsible for paying.

5. **What purpose does the cost center report serve?**

    a.   It outlines the hospital's assets, liabilities, and net worth.

    b.   It outlines the unit's assets, liabilities, and net worth.

    c.   It summarizes the hospital's revenue and expense activities.

    d.   It summarizes the unit's revenue and expense activities.

6. **The nurse manager controls and is responsible for certain expenses. Which of the following expenses does the nurse manager control?**

    a.   Revenue

    b.   Unit activity levels

    c.   Staffing

    d.   Types of staff benefits

7. **_____ costs allows you to estimate the end-of-the-year, or YTD, numbers based on the unit's monthly history.**

    a.   Annualizing

    b.   Fixing

    c.   Averaging

    d.   Multiplying

8. **Which of the following is NOT a common unit of measurement in the hospital?**

    a.   Number of procedures

    b.   Number of treatments

    c.   Total patient days

    d.   Number of insurance claims processed

9. **The breakeven analysis is important because it ultimately helps you determine:**

   a. The acuity levels of patients on the nursing unit

   b. The financial feasibility of keeping the unit open

   c. The budgeted average daily census

   d. The effect of indirect costs such as bills for electricity, copy machines, and phone

10. **Who is ultimately responsible for maintaining and updating the position control?**

   a. The chief nursing officer

   b. The unit manager or director

   c. Human resources department

   d. House supervisors

11. **To control costs on your unit, use orientation as a probationary period to weed out poor performers. Do this by evaluating new hires' performance at 30 and _____ days.**

   a. 60

   b. 90

   c. 120

   d. 150

12. **Developing goals and objectives is one part of business planning. When writing such goals, be sure they _____.**

   a. are result-oriented

   b. have a specific time frame with completion date

   c. start with "to" and are followed by an action verb

   d. specifically outline a single result

13. **Why is ROI an important part of the cost/benefit analysis?**

   a. It tells when the project/product becomes manageable.

   b. It tells when the project/product begins.

   c. It tells when the project/product becomes profitable.

   d. It tells when the project/product ends.

14. Which of the following is NOT a component of a typical business plan?

a. The executive summary

b. The identification of the problem

c. The financial implications

d. The position control

15. The _____ _____ is a snapshot of the hospital's financial picture at a certain point in time. This includes assets, liabilities, and net worth.

a. The income statement

b. The cost center report

c. The balance sheet

d. The position control

16. The breakeven analysis is important because:

a. It allows the manager to determine breakeven staffing

b. It allows the manager to maximize on revenue production

c. It allows finance to keep tabs on the manager

d. It is required by The Joint Commission

17. A full time equivalent (FTE) is comprised of all of the following except:

a. One staff member that works full time

b. One staff member that works part time

c. Two staff members who job share and together comprise a full-time position

d. More than one staff members that, together, comprise a full time position

18. Managing finances is an important part of the manager or director's job description because:

a. The insurance companies require it

b. The unions require monthly reports on staffing

c. Units or areas for which managers are responsible are contributors to the hospital's bottom line

d. Staff are costly and it is important to keep tabs on staff salaries

19. One of the biggest differences between managing a nursing department and an ancillary department is:

    a.   Nurses are harder to manage

    b.   Inpatient nursing uses patient day as the unit of service

    c.   Nursing is the only department that truly works 24 hours per day

    d.   There are no differences

20. The definition of productivity is:

    a.   Input divided by output

    b.   Hours minus patient days

    c.   How well you do on your staffing at the end of the day

    d.   Output divided by input

Continuing education evaluation

Name: _____

Title: _____

Facility name: _____

Address: _____

Address: _____

City: _____ State: _____ ZIP: _____

Phone number: _____ Fax number: _____

E-mail: _____

Nursing license number: _____

(ANCC requires a unique identifier for each learner.)

Date completed: _____

1. **This activity met the learning objectives stated:**

    Strongly Agree   Agree   Disagree   Strongly Disagree

2. **Objectives were related to the overall purpose/goal of the activity:**

    Strongly Agree   Agree   Disagree   Strongly Disagree

3. **This activity was related to my continuing education needs:**

    Strongly Agree   Agree   Disagree   Strongly Disagree

4. **The exam for the activity was an accurate test of the knowledge gained:**

    Strongly Agree   Agree   Disagree   Strongly Disagree

5. **The activity avoided commercial bias or influence:**

    Strongly Agree   Agree   Disagree   Strongly Disagree

6. **This activity met my expectations:**

    Strongly Agree   Agree   Disagree   Strongly Disagree

7. **Will this activity enhance your professional practice?**

    Yes   No

8. **The format was an appropriate method for delivery of the content for this activity:**

    Strongly Agree   Agree   Disagree   Strongly Disagree

9. **If you have any comments on this activity please note them here:**

10. **How much time did it take for you to complete this activity?**

Thank you for completing this evaluation of our continuing education activity!

Return completed form to:

HCPro, Inc. · Attention: Continuing Education Manager · 75 Sylvan Street, Suite A-101, Danvers, MA 01923

Telephone: 877/727-1728 · Fax: 781/639-2982

Relief
from all your nurse manager headaches is now just a click away!

Introducing **StrategiesforNurseManagers.com,**

a new Web site designed to help you succeed as a manager.

Check back regularly for:

- A library of customizable tools and downloadable forms
- An evidence-based resource center
- Hot-off-the-press issues and archives of the newsletter, *Strategies for Nurse Managers*
- Benchmarking reports
- A blog where you can network with your peers
- And much, much more

Log on today and click your nurse manager headaches away!

www.StrategiesforNurseManagers.com